Consciousness is Truth

The World is an Illusion

notionpress
.com

Consciousness is Truth

THE WORLD IS AN ILLUSION

SAI PRASAD NANDURI

notionpress.com

Notion Press

Old No. 38, New No. 6

McNichols Road, Chetpet

Chennai - 600 031

First Published by Notion Press 2016

ISBN 978-93-5206-625-4

DEDICATION

This work is dedicated to the cause of establishing peace and harmony in the world by transforming the people, and not by changing the environment in the name of development.

Sai Prasad Nanduri

CONTENTS

PREFACE

All living beings that are born on this Earth strive to lead a happy life. But, little analysis shows that this happiness is temporary in nature because unhappy moments always surround few happy moments. Animals might content with such transient happiness, but man, with his inquisitive nature, can imagine the happiness that lasts for ever. This state is known as Bliss, which is the goal of human beings, and can be achieved in the current life if they make a determined effort. Just like a child looks for only toys, and not for gold or diamond; an ignorant man looks for only sensual pleasures in this materialistic world, and not liberation. This book is all about achieving this goal of Bliss and liberation.

In this universe we observe only three things: The God, who is responsible for this creation, the physical world (space, time and matter), and the observer, which includes each one of us.

Philosophers, around the globe, pondered for over centuries to understand the nature of God, who is behind the creation of this world comprising of living beings and non-living things. They succeeded in disciplining the society by inculcating the fear of God in the minds of its citizens. They conceptualised God who is in heaven, punishing the wrong doers and rewarding virtuous. But, in the process, they created many religions, with conflicting philosophies, which divided the societies and nations across the continents. The history of religious conflicts around the world is an ample proof. Therefore, the philosophers could not achieve their goal because of their limited knowledge about the nature of God.

Scientists, too, have been exploring the objective world, from atomic level to cosmic level, for the last four centuries, to understand the cause of creation of this universe and life.

They are trying to understand the forces of nature, and how they control various phenomena taking place in this universe. For this, scientists plan to combine the four forces of nature into a single Super force that can reveal the Truth behind this creation. Today, what scientists could understand is less than five percent about the working of the universe. They are far away from the goal.

Through the application of science and technology, scientists are able to provide comforts to the people at large, however, the bad consequences, behind these comforts, are slowly coming to surface; global warming and damage to the delicate ecological balance of our environment that are threatening the survival of our future generations. Therefore, both philosophers and scientists could not achieve their goals, and also failed in alleviating man from his sufferings.

There is another group of explorers who are known as the spiritualists. They feel that spirituality is the common thread connecting all religions, and people must adore. This spiritual knowledge is different from the objective knowledge that is provided by the present day sciences. The spiritual knowledge is known as the subjective knowledge. The 'knowing about the knower' is known as meta-cognition, but our ancient Rishis recognised this as the knowledge of the Self. Therefore, spiritualists feel that all the efforts in trying know about the objective world without knowing about oneself will be futile.

Right from the beginning of industrial revolution, philosophers realized there are only two modes of developing the society: One is to change the environment around us, so that life becomes secure and comfortable; the second one is to change the mind and attitude of man of the society, so that he can live in peace and harmony with nature. Unfortunately we opted for the first choice for the sake of comforts, and today, we changed our environment so drastically that our future generations might find it difficult to survive. Therefore, the solution lies in changing the mind of man and his attitude so that he and his society can live in peace and harmony with nature. This can be achieved only by imparting spiritual knowledge or Self-knowledge.

How was this 'Self-Knowledge' discovered? The Rishis of ancient India could define God as Absolute phenomenon behind this world, who is Eternal, Infinite and Knowledge. By serious contemplation, and through intuitive knowledge, they could infer that the observable universe, comprising of space, time, matter and living beings, is continuously undergoing changes, and therefore, cannot be real, whereas what is Eternal shall not undergo any changes, nor divisible into parts. Since all planets are moving around the sun, and the sun is moving around the galaxy, and galaxies are moving away from each other, it is difficult to search for the Ultimate Reality in the objective world we live in.

They also noticed that human mind is also undergoing changes while passing from one conscious state to another; from waking state of the day, we go to dream state and then to deep-sleep state in the night, and this cycle is repeated. By contemplating over decades, many Rishis came to the conclusion that the Truth must lie as the substratum and witness to these three changing conscious states. This substratum is nothing but Pure Consciousness.

Suppose, we take a man, blind folded, on to the moon, in a rocket, without his knowledge, and unfold him. During the first few moments, his mind will not be active, void of any thoughts, and he does not know where he is. This conscious experience, during the first few moments is known as Pure Consciousness. After a while his mind starts functioning, and by comparison, he will slowly come to know he is not on the earth. It is a fact that all living beings enjoy maximum happiness during deep-sleep than any other occasion, since mind is not active during deep-sleep.

The Rishis have contemplated on the nature of mind and its faculties that resulted in the Self-knowledge. This knowledge is such, when once known, one feels he need not know anything else. For this reason, it is called Highest Knowledge or Truth. This is not a mental state that can be reached neither by pills or drugs, nor by yoga or meditation, but only through Self-knowledge,

The world of plurality is only a projection, and a created thing cannot be different from the material from which it is created. Thus the Creator and the created world are not two separate factors. The created universe is yet another form of the Creator, just like the ornaments made out of gold cannot be different from the gold. This non-duality is the Highest Truth as propounded by Sankaracharya through his Advaita philosophy.

It has been found that the root cause for all ills faced by man in the society is man himself and his mind that creates duality. The true nature of man is Blissful Consciousness. As long as one is ignorant, he suffers in this world. This Self-knowledge can be gained by a person, with sharp intellect, by distinguishing what is real and what is unreal in this observable universe in a systematic way.

The man of Self-Realisation enjoys the following four-fold benefits:

1. He will remain happy ever after.
2. He will involve in worldly affairs and family matters without getting entangled.
3. He overcomes fear of death and diseases.
4. He dies only once.

(N.S. PRASAD)

ACKNOWLEDGEMENT

I am extremely grateful and indebted to Swami Paripoornananda Saraswati of Sree Peetham, Kakinada, A.P., whose teachings, I have recorded and heard repeatedly, are the inspiration for writing this book. I happened to meet him twice, though for a very short time. I felt as a miracle when he agreed to write foreword for this book.

I am indebted to Late. Sri SitaramaYathindrulu of Pedamuktevi, AP who was my Father's Guru, introduced me to education at the age of 5 by performing a ceremony, and also blessed me personally by his graceful presence, during my wedding. His miraculous presence at the last hour of my father's death still fascinates me.

I am indebted to Late Sri AdiSankaracharya, the founder of the Advaita Philosophy on which this book is based. I am also grateful to AdvaitaAshrama, Kolkata, for bringing out English translations of important Upanishads with Commentary by Sri AdiSankaracharya. Without these books I could not have ventured into writing this book.

I am ever grateful to the above enlightened Souls, and revere them as Gurus in daily prayers.

I am thankful to my friends Mr.S.Hiriyanna, and Mr. B. Chithambaram, and my eldest brother, Dr. N.G. Rao for their encouragement and suggestions.

AUTHOR

FOREWORD

The journey of life attains meaning and profundity when one is able to clearly distinguish between the real and the unreal, the spiritual and the corporal and consciousness and illusion.

The great sage Adi Sankaracharya expressed this sagaciously and concisely in his Advaita philosophy when he said: "Brahma Satyam; Jagat Mithya" meaning "Only God is Real, rest is unreal."

From the earth's perspective, the Sun rises in the East and sets in the West but if we consider the solar system as a whole, there is no Sun rise or Sun set – only the ever glowing Sun. This is the Absolute Reality. What we observe from earth is empirical reality.

There is only one Absolute phenomenon in this Universe, the Supreme Consciousness, which we call God who is all-pervasive. This truth can be realized through self-knowledge, by careful scrutiny and contemplation that the world comprising space, time and matter and human beings comprising the physical body, senses, mind, intellect and ego are all unreal.

Consciousness is very sublime and helps us in merely knowing the physical properties of living and non-living objects around. One's aim, however, should be to discover Pure Consciousness, the substratum of all existence, in contrast to the materialistic world which is merely a super-imposition by the mind.

I am happy Prof. Sai Prasad Nanduri, a former scientist at the Indian Space Research Organisation (ISRO), inspired by my teachings, has ventured into writing this book "Consciousness is Truth; the World is an Illusion." He has combined his deep knowledge of science with spirituality in a laudable effort to understand the cause of creation of this universe and life.

I am confident this book will resonate with a wide range of readers and help them gain better knowledge of the self towards fulfilment of the goal of realising a state of bliss, not just transient happiness.

My blessings are with him for the success of this endeavour.

Sri Swami Paripoornananda Saraswati
Sree Peetham, Kakinada
01-01-2016

INTRODUCTION

We are all generally caught up with much of the time with worldly pursuits, sensual gratifications, gross entertainment and enjoyment, meeting the demands of life. If we make our mind free, what we observe, today, in the present world, is the extremism in all walks of life. The peaceful society is threatened with extremists from all sides. Terrorism, rapes, intolerance to religious beliefs of another community, nuclear missiles, greed, climate change and global warming, droughts, floods, accidents, etc. Of all these extremes, what causes serious concern to the society is that anger, greed, jealousy, hatred, lust, violence which are reaching their limits. The world is going to witness cultural wars over religious beliefs, shortage of food and water in addition to border disputes. It is often said, when the unrighteousness in the society reaches the extreme, then only is the beginning of time of coming to an end of it, due to some social, economic or natural catastrophe.

The solution lies in transforming the mindset of people at large. This can happen only by imparting the right knowledge. Man is trying to go to the extremes in all field of knowledge to earn livelihood, but he is ignoring to know about his true nature. He is living without any purpose in life, forgetting that all species who live on this planet try to maximise their happiness. The Self-knowledge alone brings man self-control, peace of mind, equipoise, and eternal bliss.

God or Brahman is only one, even though people of different faiths worship him in different names and forms. He is absolute. We observe, in the world, anything that has name or form would perish one day or other. One can also observe, in this, so-called God created universe, nothing is eternal. Even stars are born and die after a fixed life span. This is true of anything we observe in this universe. Even the universe was not there in the beginning, and it will be dissolved one day. Only God is eternal.

'A thing that does not exist in the beginning, and does not exist at the end, cannot exist in the middle'. This is the law of unreality as stated in Mandukya Upanishad. Therefore, God must be absolute, formless, nameless and timeless.

We feel and experience this world as real. However, according to the law of causality, an effect can never be brought about by a cause in isolation. For example, to create a pot, the potter himself is not enough; he needs clay, potter's wheel, water and things. These are called contributory causes.

Before the creation of the universe only God existed and nothing else; it means no other cause existed except God. In that case how did God produce anything? If God had created this universe, he must have a *desire* to do so, and also a *purpose*. Such attributes are not the characteristics of God. Therefore, nothing can be produced or created by God; the world must be illusory in nature, and it cannot be different from God. Cause and effect are not two separate processes, but two aspects of the same process. There is no difference between a seed and sprout; fire and heat, Karma and Man.

When we pause for a moment and ponder over the greatness of ancient sciences, called Vedas, we wonder at their range and perfection and the cyclopaedia of knowledge. The Vedas reflect the life and world of the glorious age of Aryans. It is the expression of their knowledge wherein we find that all individual science, not only highly developed, but also, they enter into a coherent system of thought which resulted in the unqualified knowledge known under the title "Veda."

All sciences, arts, astronomy, mathematics, grammar, medicine, war, poetry, phonetics and music, etc. will find their respective places in this system as different branches. Above all, at the very centre, there is epistemology or the science of knowledge which justifies the name Veda. Vedas are meant only to guide the man as how to conduct himself during his present life, defines his goal of life, and teaches him how to reach. From the knowledge of this integral system of sciences, it appears that the Aryans explored life, and lived an active and contented life in all its aspects; spiritual, intellectual and materialistic. The ancient Rishis were original in their thought and language. The creative power of their thoughts burst out into natural free flowing expressions. This is how the Vedas were originated.

Modern sciences, as we know to day, branched off from philosophy, some 400 years ago. Philosophy evolved into metaphysics which eventually became physics and branched off into different sciences such as chemistry, biology, botany, zoology, astronomy, mathematics, sociology, logic, applied sciences and so on. Today we call them in the name of science and technology. Not only physics branched off into variety of disciplines, the nations got divided into different societies based on different faiths, despite the fact that God is only one. Nations also got divided into, developed and under-developed, based on distribution of natural resources and economic development.

The basic survival needs like food, water and air were provided by Nature. With advances in science and technology, we are provided with more comforts. But these comforts which everyone is enjoying today comes at a price; of damaging our own environment and ecology. We can say man's conquest of nature is brilliant, but the misuse of his victory is turning tragic. Today, we are living under constant threat of nature's fury and diseases, due to climate change that are threatening our existence.

The need of the hour is to integrate all disciplines of science into one branch so that unified law can be discovered which can explain the working of the universe right from subatomic level up to the cosmos. Similarly, there is a need to forge diverse societies practicing different faiths into one mould. This is possible only if humanity at large, adopts to spirituality that unites different societies, moving and raising above their religious faiths which are dividing nations and society.

To move towards these goals, requires an unbiased comparison between science and spirituality, and to discover the highest truth which enlightens man and make him happy, which is the goal of humanity. This book is planned towards complete knowledge which alone can make man happy ever after, and not the comforts. To gain this knowledge one must have sharp intellect, and wisdom to distinguish between what is real and unreal, and what is true and untrue, in both science and spirituality.

This highest Knowledge is important for two reasons: Our thoughts depend upon our knowledge, our attitude depends on our thoughts, our behaviour depends on our attitude, and finally our destiny depends on our behaviour. Secondly happiness is a state of our mind, which, in turn, depends on our knowledge.

In this book, starting from the knowledge of science, what we know today, a systematic effort is made to prove that Truth is only one that is but Pure Consciousness, and everything else is not real. Present day scientists are assuming that life and consciousness evolved from inert matter, which is refuted in this book based on what was established 2000 years ago by Adi Sankaracharya.

ORIGIN OF OUR UNIVERSE

Our universe is so vast to imagine. It is estimated that there are 100 billion galaxies in our universe, and each galaxy housing about 100 billion stars like our sun.

The most popular theory about the origin of our universe which is valid as on today is known as the 'big bang theory'. According to this theory, our universe was created from a big explosion. This theory was born of the observation that other galaxies are moving away from our own galaxy, Milky Way, at great speed, in all directions, as if they had all been propelled by an explosive force. This expanding universe was discovered by measuring what is known as the 'red shift' effect.

Our universe is estimated to have originated about 14 billion years ago from a singularity with high temperature and density. The temperature, before start of the big bang, is estimated to be of the order of 10^{28} K, and due to expansion of the universe, the present temperature of the deep space has been estimated and measured in the year 1965 and found to be 2.7 K and is known as the cosmic background radiation temperature. The Bing Bang Model about the origin of universe is partially validated. It may be mentioned that prior to the Big Bang theory, Steady State Universe theory was prevailing; that is without any expansion whatsoever.

A Belgian priest named Georges Lemaitre first suggested the big bang theory in the 1920s. He theorized that the universe began from a single primordial atom. The idea subsequently received major boosts by Edwin Hubble's observations that galaxies are speeding away from us in all directions, and from the discovery of cosmic microwave radiation by Arno Penzias and Robert Wilson. The glow of cosmic microwave background radiation, which is found throughout the universe, is thought to be a tangible remnant of leftover light from the big bang. It is supposed to be the oldest radiation known and may hold many secrets about the universe's earliest moments.

The universe, before explosion, measured only few millimetres across with a density of about 10^{73} g/cc and consisted of high temperature plasma. The universe, in such a state, suddenly exploded with a bang and started spewing radiation, probably comprising of quark-gluon plasma, in all directions.

This theory maintains that, in the instant—a trillion-trillionth of a second—after the big bang, the universe expanded with incomprehensible speed from its pebble-size origin to astronomical scale. Expansion has apparently continued, but much more slowly, over the ensuing billions of years. It is like blowing up a balloon, as you blow air in, the exterior of the balloon expands outward.

When this radiation cooled, gradually, matter started appearing starting with hydrogen. The hydrogen clouds later collapsed under gravity and formed into stars triggering nuclear fusion reactions. Clusters of stars formed into galaxies. The higher elements were formed inside the stars due to fusion, and when the star explodes, such as in the case of supernova, the higher elements are thrown into outer space which enabled to form the planets like our earth.

The Big Bang theory depends on two major assumptions: the universality of physical laws and the cosmological principle. The first assumption is that the laws of physics discovered so far are valid throughout the universe. The cosmological principle states that on large scales the universe is homogeneous and isotropic.

The formation of a universe must be such that it must be hospitable to support intelligent life. This, however, depends on a number of physical constants. Because we are intelligent beings, we are, by definition, in a hospitable universe. The constants that decide the fate of a universe include universal gravitational constant. If this constant varied by just one in 10^{60} parts, none of us would exist. Similarly, other parameters include critical energy density, the cosmological constant, which describes the ratio of the density of dark energy to the critical energy density of the universe, the ratio of strength of electromagnetic force to gravitational force, and the ratio of mass of electron to that of proton to name a few.

Aleksey Filipino, the American astrophysicist, who won Nobel Prize in 2011, stated that what scientists know about our universe is only 4.6%. This is what is known as the visible universe. The unknown universe is found to comprise of 23% dark matter and72.4% dark energy; these are yet to be explored. It is known that dark matter attracts other matter while the dark energy repels matter. The present universe is undergoing accelerated expansion which means that galaxies are receding from each other with increasing speed. The latest findings support the view that the universe is heading for a slow death.

Once it was understood that the Universe had a beginning, scientists began to ask how it did come into existence, and what existed before it?"

Most scientists now believe that the answer to the first part of the question is that the Universe sprang into existence from a singularity - a term physicists use to describe regions of space that defy the laws of physics. We know very little about singularities, but most scientists believe that such singularities probably exist in the cores of all black holes. The second part of the question, as to what existed before the Big Bang, has scientists baffled. By definition, nothing existed prior to the beginning of singularity, but this fact creates more questions than answers. For instance, if nothing existed prior to the Big Bang, what is the cause for the singularity to come into existence in the first place?

The big bang theory leaves several major questions unanswered. One is the original cause of the big bang itself. Several theories have been proposed to address this fundamental question, but none has been proven—and even adequately testing them is proving to be a formidable challenge. For Scientists, the origin of the universe is one of the unanswered questions.

Origin of Our Sun

After the Big- Bang, as the radiation cooled further, resulted in the formation of large hydrogen clouds. These clouds started contracting due to their own gravity. This contraction resulted into heat generation, forming a ball of fire. When the temperature had risen to millions of degrees, nuclear reactions began which converted hydrogen into helium, and as a result stars like our sun have formed. Two atomic nuclei of hydrogen and neutrons combined to form helium. This process was accompanied by release of large amount of energy. Our sun was formed about 4.5 billion years ago. It might shine for another 4.5 billion years.

This exceptional life of our sun is attributed to the delicate balance of its thermal pressure and gravity. The Milky Way galaxy in which our solar system is located contains about 200 billion stars, and our galaxy is situated inside Virgo Cluster which contains 2500 galaxies like our Milky Way. The sun, with its planets, goes round the Milky Way once in 10^8 years.

The Sun is the star at the centre of the Solar System and is by far the most important source of energy for life on Earth. It is nearly a perfect spherical ball of hot gases, and the convective motion of ionized gases in the core generates a magnetic field. Its diameter is about 109 times that of Earth, and it has a mass about 0.3 million times that of Earth. About three quarters of the Sun's mass consists of hydrogen; the rest is mostly helium, with much smaller quantities of heavier elements, including oxygen, carbon, neon and iron. However, after hydrogen fuel in its core gets exhausted, the Sun will undergo severe changes and become a red giant. It is calculated that the Sun will become sufficiently large in size to engulf the present orbits of planets, Mercury, Venus and Earth. This might take another 4 billion years from now.

The core of the sun extends to about 25% of its radius, and has a temperature of about 7 million K, while its surface temperature drops to 5800 K. Sunlight is Earth's primary source of energy. The nuclear fuels such as uranium, found on earth, is due to nuclear redactions in stars like our sun and thrown into space during explosion of the stars, and caught by planets like earth. These fissionable nuclear materials are trapped in Earth's crust. Some of these give rise to geothermal energy, which drives the volcanism on earth.

The solar constant is the amount of radiated power that the Sun deposits per unit area on the part of the earth that is directly exposed to sunlight. The solar constant is equal to, approximately, 1,368 W/m^{2}. Sunlight on the surface of Earth is attenuated by Earth's atmosphere so that less power arrives at the surface—closer to 1,000 W/m^{2} in clear conditions when the Sun is near the zenith. Sunlight at the top of Earth's atmosphere is composed (by total energy) of about 50% infrared light, 40% visible light, and 10% ultraviolet light. The atmosphere, in particular, filters out over 70% of solar ultraviolet, especially, at the shorter wavelengths. This radiation is responsible for ionizing the gases in the upper atmosphere of earth and creating what is known a conducting ionosphere.

When the nuclear reactions cease due to exhausting of hydrogen fuel, the pressure inside most of the stars gets reduced and the gravitational force will become dominant. This gravitational contraction further raises the temperature and causes the helium to burn. Three nuclei of helium combine to form one nucleus of carbon. Since, helium burns more rapidly than hydrogen, the thermal pressure within the star increases and the star starts expanding again. At this stage, rarefied matter, consisting of hot and dense un-burnt hydrogen, envelopes the burning helium within. Astronomers call such stars as Red Giants.

The collapsed core might become a white dwarf, comprising of degenerate matter which forced two electrons to occupy the same space. A star more massive than our Sun eventually becomes a neutron star via a similar process. Still more massive stars collapse to form black holes. This is how most of the stars like our sun end up.

Every star has birth, life and death. Some giant stars, after all the helium fuel is exhausted, they lose their stability and explode forming so-called Supernova." This supernova explosion spewed heavy elements mixed with hydrogen into the space. Thus all chemical elements we find on earth today were synthesised in stars and distributed all over space. The subsequent generation of stars like our sun, formed from hydrogen had from the very outset, an admixture of heavy elements.

The proposition that the material of the earth was indeed derived from an exploding star - a supernova, is supported by strong evidence. The shower of stars must have been surrounded by a cloud of gas - the cloud from which the stars had just condensed. A supernova, undergoing violent disintegration, must have expelled gases that went to join this cloud, the material from the supernova thereby getting mixed with the large quantity of hydrogen of which the cloud was mainly composed. The present problem is then to explain how both the sun and the planets were formed out of this mixture of materials.

Had the mass of our sun more than its present mass, it would not have lived this long, and would have ended up as a neutron star, white dwarf or a black hole. The planets would not have been formed. Similarly had the mass of sun is less it would not have lived this long. This long life of nearly

9 billion years is attributed to its mass and radius that decide it's gravitational force.

Origin of Earth

The age of Earth is approximately one-third of the age of the universe. An immense amount of biological and geological change has occurred in that time span. Earth formed around 4.5 billion years ago by accretion from the solar nebula. Volcanic outgassing probably created the primordial atmosphere, but it contained almost no oxygen and would have been toxic to most forms of life. Much of the Earth was molten because of frequent collisions with other bodies which led to extreme volcanic activity. One very large collision is thought to have been responsible for tilting the Earth at an angle and forming the Moon. Over time, the planet cooled and formed a solid crust, allowing liquid water to exist on the surface. How the oceans came into existence remains a mystery, not completely resolved even today. Life is made possible on earth because of solar energy and oceans.

Earth is our home in the vast expanse of space. Earth is the only planet which harbours life in the entire solar system or probably in the Milky Way Galaxy. It is at a distance of 1.5×10^{8} km from the sun that sustains life on earth. Earth has a radius of 6400 km with a mass of 5.9×10^{24} kg. The planet's mass and its positions from the sun were the factors that decided the composition of the planet and its atmosphere as they condensed under their gravitational force. Except Earth, Mercury, Venus and Mars all other planets are gaseous in nature with no continents like on earth.

Many cosmologists believe that originally the atmosphere of all planets in our solar system was similar in composition to that of the sun consisting primarily hydrogen, helium along with other higher chemical elements. Small amount of methane, ammonia, water vapour, carbon dioxide and nitrogen were present. In the process of planet formation most of the lighter gases like hydrogen, helium escaped into space as the gravity of earth is very less compared to the sun. Out of all the planets, only earth could retain the atmosphere which is essential to the formation of life.

The planets which are farther away from the sun do not receive enough solar radiation, and the freezing temperatures could not support life. Similarly the planets closer to the sun than earth could not support life as the surface temperatures are so high. In the case where the planet's mass was more than the earth the solar radiation could not penetrate their dense atmosphere retained by virtue of high gravitational force. On the contrary, the planets whose masses were less than the earth could not retain the atmosphere that is needed for life, because of their poor gravitational forces.

A number of other conditions that are essential for the life sustaining processes on earth are: the rotation of earth about its own axis causing day and night of approximately equal duration that is required for cooling and heating alternately that is needed to drive the winds around the globe. Earth's spin about a tilted axis is responsible for the formation of seasons. The rotation of the earth around the sun keeping appropriate distance is responsible to keep water in liquid form. Four major elements, hydrogen, carbon, nitrogen and oxygen constitute most of the organisms on our planet. Other higher elements that are deposited on the earth had their origin in the nuclear reactions in stars which later exploded through supernova.

Origin of Life

Prior to the origin of life, the earth was comprised of lifeless oceans, Rocky Mountains, and atmosphere containing water vapour, methane, ammonia and hydrogen. Only powerful lightening and volcanic eruptions disturbed the silence. Since the ozone layer was not formed due to the absence of oxygen, the short wave UV radiation reached freely the surface of the earth, and life could not evolve. Then came into existence molecules of sugar, nitrogenous bases and other simple carbon based molecules, from which complex proteins, nuclei acids, fats and energy carrying substances such as adenosine triphosphate were formed. Sparks of thunder discharges were found to be adequate to form amino acids from a mixture of methane, ammonia, hydrogen and water. The most elaborate theory concerned with the coacervate (microscopic lipid molecule) stage in the development of life has been advanced by A.I. Operon.

There are number of other theories but few with clear facts. The first theory proposed was that life evolved in oceans and gradually encroached on to the land as the atmosphere became suitable. Another theory proposes that life evolved on land, since fossilised life forms were discovered in some old forms. However, the most compelling hypothesis is that life formed elsewhere in the space, but transported to earth through comets or meteorites. The evidence for earliest life forms came from the discovery, in Western Australia, of microbial fossils in the meta-sedimentary rocks dated to be some 3.8 billion-year – old.

Photosynthetic life appeared around 2 billion years ago, enriching the atmosphere with oxygen. Life remained mostly small and microscopic until about 580 million years ago, when complex multicellular life arose. During the Cambrian period it experienced a rapid diversification into most major phyla. More than 99 percent of all species, amounting to over five billion species that ever lived on Earth are estimated to be extinct. Estimates on the number of Earth's current species range from 10 million to 14 million, of which about 1.2 million have been documented and over 86 percent have not yet been described.

Geological change has been constantly occurring on Earth since the time of its formation and biological change since the first appearance of life. Species continuously evolve, taking on new forms, splitting into daughter species, or going extinct in response to an ever-changing planet. The process of plate tectonics must have played a major role in the shaping of Earth's oceans and continents, as well as the life they harbour. The biosphere, in turn, has had a significant effect on the atmosphere and other abiotic conditions on the planet, such as the formation of the ozone layer, the proliferation of oxygen, and the creation of soil.

There are a number of hypotheses which attempt to explain the origin of life on earth. The first and the oldest of these hypotheses suggest that life was created by a Supreme Being or a Spiritual force. Many religions around the world believe in this even today. The second hypotheses suggest that life began in another part of the universe and arrived on earth by chance through a meteor or a comet. The third, and most widely accepted hypothesis in the scientific community, is that life began approximately 3.5 billion years ago as a result of complex sequence of chemical reactions that took place spontaneously in Earth's atmosphere. In the 1950's two biochemists explained that certain molecules of life (amino acids) could form spontaneously under the right conditions of atmosphere. These molecules interacted with one another eventually resulting in the earliest forms of life.

From the existence of molecules of sugar, amino acids, nitrogenous bases and simple carbon containing molecules from which complex proteins, nuclei acids, fats and energy carrying substance such as adenosine triphosphate were formed. This must have taken at least billion years. Life seems to have been evolved from the very beginning as a cycle of substances based on the interaction of photo-autotrophy and heterotrophy. The only source of energy for these processes is solar radiation. A significant stage in the evolution of life is the formation of individual organisms showing considerable variety in metabolism.

Active photosynthesis by plankton must have produced great quantities of oxygen in the atmosphere, which later transformed into ozone. This ozone layer prevented the dangerous ultraviolet radiation of the sun from reaching the earth. The life formation thereafter was exciting. First came the single cell bacteria, then multicellular bacteria such as algae. Then the evolution followed quickly starting from fish, reptile, flying reptiles, birds, dinosaurs and finally mammals like monkeys. This must have happened 0.5 billion years ago. Thus living organisms, from the lowest form to the highest form were evolved, and resulted in the extension of life on to the land.

The origin of life, as on today, remains still a mystery yet to be solved by scientists. Many attempts to create life in the laboratory were proved futile. This remains as one of the goals of science after the origin of universe.

1

EVOLUTION OF HUMAN BEING

1.1 EVOLUTION OF LIFE

There are three distinct theories about evolution of different life forms on earth. As per the foremost, which was consistent with Darwin's theory of evolution, life evolved on earth, most probably in the seas, from a primordial soup comprising of ammonia, carbon dioxide, methane, water vapour and hydrogen. It gradually evolved from lower forms to higher forms: single cell, multicellular-bacteria, fish, reptiles, birds, mammals and finally man. The evolution that proceeded for millions of years was fundamentally guided by two principles: random mutations and natural selection.

There was yet another theory postulated by a Russian scientist: Life did not evolve in the sea, but evolved on land. This theory was based on the discovery of fossilized skeletons of different life forms discovered beneath rocks that were dated as old as 3.5 billion years. This theory differs with the earlier theory only on the question of as how initially life forms came into existence. On the question of evolution, this theory is consistent with Darwin's theory of natural selection.

Francis Crick, a biologist and a Nobel laureate, who was famous for his discovery of DNA, proposed a hypothesis that life might have evolved in deep cosmos and transported to earth through meteorites. He studied major ingredients of life, 20 amino acids, four nucleotides and the particular combination that could result in the evolution of life. Since experiments in the laboratory to evolve life proved futile, he opined that life could not have evolved on earth purely based on probability. If one were to evolve life in a test tube, trying all possible 10^{30} combinations involving essential ingredients, it would probably take scientists billions of years and the present age of the earth, taking all factors into account, would not have been adequate to allow life to evolve. Latest studies on fossilized species indicate that life, probably, evolved around 4.0 billion years ago, whereas earth was formed about 4.5 billion years ago. Obviously this short span of 0.5 billion years is not adequate for complex life forms to evolve. He finally concluded that life evolved in outer space, and transported by meteorites onto earth. This was supported by scientists like Fred Hoyle who established the feasibility of life surviving the ordeals of space journey and withstanding earth's re-entry temperature.

However, no theory, so far, is complete and convincing and there are a number of unanswered questions relating to fundamental properties of life: highly ordered structure, regulation of metabolism with complex control system, and self-reproduction, etc.

Charles Darwin, Jean Lamarck, Mendel, S. Wright, A.I. Operon, E.S. Bower, Albert Szent Gyorgyi were the famous scientists who were involved in the study of life's evolution. Darwin's theory of evolution is widely accepted even today.

Ever since Francis Crick and James Watson discovered DNA, lot of secrets of life were revealed. The cell is the only material system known to possess all properties of life such as self-regulation and reproduction. The cell contains imprinted genetic information which is the result of millions of years of evolutionary development of species and the basis for the whole of its future evolution. The cell is a complex and intricate system made up of two main components: the nucleus and cytoplasm. The nucleus contains chromosomes, nucleons and nuclear sap and is enclosed by a two layer porous membrane separating it from cytoplasm. The cytoplasm is a transparent fluid comprising mitochondria, ribosomes and other organoids. The chemical composition of the cell comprises 70% water, ions of various salts, proteins, nucleic acids, fat like substances known as lipids and carbohydrates. The carbohydrates serve in building biopolymers like amino acids and nucleotides, and accumulate energy. Proteins are compounds directly involved in metabolism. Enzymes are biological catalysts of protein and are involved in the synthesis and decomposition of food and release of energy.

Another group of compounds are nucleic acids which are basically biopolymers. These are two types: deoxyribonucleic acid (DNA) and ribonucleic acid (RNA). The DNA comprises of two polymer (nucleotides) strands coiled around each other into a double helix, resembling a twisted ladder with side pieces made of sugar and phosphates and closely spaced rungs. Each rung is called a base pair and comprises of complimentary chemicals called nitrogenous bases, attached end to end; either adenine (A) joined to thymine (T) or cytosine(C) attached to guanine (G). The fundamental property of DNA is the fact that A and T are mutually attractive, and so is the pair C and G. Another remarkable feature of DNA is that each of the four bases represent a letter in the genetic code and contains instructions to cell on how to assemble amino acids into proteins essential to the structure and life of its host.

Each complete DNA sentence is called a gene, a discrete segment of the DNA string, responsible for ordering the production of a specific protein. A genetic message that might read ACGGTAGAT represents the code for three of the 20 amino acids which are the important constituents of proteins. The genetic code for simple bacterium comprises of 4.5 million base pairs or letters, while the genetic message of a human being comprises of some 5 billion letters. There are about

100,000 genes in each one of us and represent coded messages comprising of 15000 to 1, 50,000 letters each. So far scientists are able to locate and decode about 300 genes.

The primary role of RNA is to convert the information stored in the DNA into proteins. But there are three different types of RNA. The messenger RNA (mRNA) carries the protein blueprint from a cell's DNA to its ribosomes, which are the "machines" that drive protein synthesis. The transfer RNA (tRNA) then carries the appropriate amino acids into the ribosome for inclusion in the new protein. Meanwhile, the ribosomes themselves consist largely of ribosomal RNA (rRNA) molecules.

Thus, RNA molecules play numerous roles in both normal cellular processes and disease states. Generally, those RNA molecules that do not take the form of mRNA are referred to as noncoding, because they do not encode proteins. The involvement of noncoding mRNAs in many regulatory processes, their abundance, and their diversity of functions has led to the hypothesis that an "RNA world" may have preceded the evolution of DNA and proteins (Gilbert, 1986).

Genetic engineering, also called genetic modification, is the direct manipulation of an organism's genome using biotechnology. It is therefore a set of technologies used to change the genetic makeup of cells, including the transfer of genes within and across species boundaries to produce new species or organisms with desired characteristics. This is known as gene cloning technology. Under this process unwanted or mutated gene can be removed and a good gene can be inserted in its place. This gene removal and inserting is done by making use of certain enzymes.

The organism realized through genetic manipulation or changes is known as Genetically Modified Organism(GMO). The first GMOs were bacteria generated in 1973 and GM mice in 1974. Scientists, in the year 1982, were able to realize insulin-producing bacteria, and in the year 1994, they realized genetically modified crops, and genetically modified food appeared in the market in the year 2003.

Genetic engineering techniques have been applied in numerous fields including research, agriculture, industrial biotechnology, and medicine. Enzymes used in laundry detergent and medicines such as insulin and human growth hormone are now manufactured in GM cells, experimental GM cell lines and GM animals such as mice and some kinds of fish are currently being used in research, and genetically modified food or crops have already been commercialised.

However, the genetic engineering has its own risks, and many countries are thinking of banning GM crops, because people are developing unknown allergies. Today, people are willing to pay more money to buy organic foods, and avoiding genetically modified foods or crops. There are also other reasons such as biodiversity will be affected, as GM crops promote monoculture.

These crops also cost more money than expected, and Asian markets are stopping to import American corn. The genetically engineered wheat created loss to the business in 2004. The genetically modified crops was encouraged mainly with the hope that it will eliminate hunger from the world. With so many problems facing, the goal remains as myth.

1.2 OUR ENVIRONMENT

The total land surface area of Earth is about 515 million square km, of which about 33% are covered by desserts; about 24% is mountainous, 30% forests. Subtracting from the total land area we get the land area available for human habitation as 67.7 million square km for the world population today of 7.5

billion. Further we require land for rivers, lakes and roads. This translates to a land of 100 x 100m per person on this planet.

Due to the rain cycle, the water from the seas, rivers and lakes evaporate into clouds, and on cooling, it comes back as rain. Unfortunately 97 percent of the rain falls back in the oceans which cannot be used. Out of this 3 percent, nearly 80 percent is available in the form of ice. The net amount of water available for agriculture and human consumption is mere 0.02 percent. Even this is not available since sufficient quantity is required to maintain the flow of rivers, and lastly the ground water that is available below 800m cannot be drawn economically.

Water resources are needed for industries producing necessary goods and also for our day to day life. For example, to get 1 litre of milk, we require 3500 litres of water for grass to grow as fodder for cattle. Similarly to produce 1 kg of rice 2500 litres of water is needed; to produce 1 kg of paper requires 700litres of water and 1 kg of steel production consumes 150 litres. If we take all these into account, the water consumption per head works out to about 500 litres per day.

Earth provided the right atmosphere for evolution of life. The atmosphere comprises of approximately 20% oxygen and 80% nitrogen. Out of all species, plants only know how to convert carbon dioxide and water into biomass with the help of sunlight and releasing oxygen into the atmosphere through a process known as photosynthesis. Because of this, a balance between plant species that take carbon dioxide and give out oxygen and species that require oxygen is maintained.

Ozone, the molecule comprising of three oxygen atoms, is available in our atmosphere at an altitude range of 20–30 km. This ozone layer, if spread out uniformly on the earth's surface, constitutes a sheet of mere 3mm thickness. This ozone layer is protecting life on earth from the harmful ultraviolet radiation coming from the sun.

For the survival of all species on this planet, natural bio-chemical cycles are important. We all know how important the rain cycle for our survival is. Similarly other cycles include elements like carbon, oxygen, nitrogen, hydrogen, and sulphur. They pass through the atmosphere in transit from one stage to another of their cycle. This mineral circulation is essential for the survival of all species on this planet, since flora and fauna, including humans, require these minerals for survival and growth.

It is interesting to analyse how we are interfering with our environment and damaging the delicate ecological balance. What we need on this planet are air to breath, water to drink and food to eat. These are the primary requirements for our survival, and are made available to us by Mother Nature.

We do not need engineers and scientists for providing these basic necessities. For life to exist, so many conditions, which are beyond the scope of scientists, must have existed. As already discussed, exact and precise force of explosion during big bang, earth's position from sun, its spin about a tilted axis, its appropriate gravitational force due to its mass and radius to hold the atmosphere; all these conditions must be satisfied for life to form and evolve on our planet. Also for life to survive on earth, we need rain cycle, oxygen cycle, carbon cycle, nitrogen cycle, ozone cycle etc. in addition to maintaining proper seasons and climate.

At present, our industrial civilisation, with burning of fossil fuels has already disturbed these cycles. There is, too, an increasingly worrying interference with the ozone cycle which is an off-shoot of oxygen cycle. The damage to our environment by indiscriminate use of technologies, and their by-products are seriously interfering with the delicate ecological balance.

1.3 OUR ECOLOGICAL SYSTEMS

Every year about 100 billion tonnes of organic matter is produced on earth by green plants through photosynthesis. An approximately equivalent amount is oxidised back to carbon dioxide and water during the same time interval. An excess organic production over respiration was a major reason for decrease in carbon dioxide and build-up of oxygen in the atmosphere. This resulted in the evolution of higher forms of life including human beings.

About 0.5 billion years' back excess organic production as well as dead organic matter, that got buried, resulted in the formation of fossil fuels like coal, oil, and natural gas. Discovery of these fossil fuels has accelerated the industrial revolution. Today, due to human actions involving deforestation and industrial development, the carbon dioxide level in the atmosphere is gradually increasing. In order to maintain the relative stability of biotic circulation, the organic matter produced by photosynthesis is to be balanced by its consumption by animals and microorganisms. Therefore, biotic circulation involving synthesis and destruction of organic matter is essential for the organisation of life on earth. The concept of life thus treats not an individual organism, but the totality of living beings that live in oceans and on lands, which are inter-related with one another in a certain way. This is known as ecology of our biosphere.

The ecological phenomena in our biosphere are governed by five variables: Matter, energy, diversity, space and time. The biomass (matter) is produced by plants through photosynthesis using sun light. All other life forms survive on this biomass. The solar energy is distributed to all species through food chain. Longer the food chain, smaller is the energy transfer. All species in an ecosystem compete with each other for space (shelter) and food for their survival. Diversity is the richness of population in a community. It is defined as the ratio of population of one community to the square root of total number of species in an ecosystem.

Complex ecosystems, with high diversity, provide greater resistance against attacks by natural forces. This can be understood by observing that trees in a rainforest survive by themselves, while the plants in our backyard have to be continually supplied with water and fertilisers or nutrients.

Stability in climate over long periods of time is essential to produce wider ecological diversity. For example, in an ecosystem where the rain cycle is affected and there will be decrease of rainfall, the diversity there decreases. We notice today, that one in six species on this planet is facing extinction due to human interference to our environment and ecosystems.

Looking at the number of conditions that have to be satisfied for the evolution of life on our planet, we are forced to believe that some super power is behind the creation of life on earth. Just as milk is made ready in mother's breast before the child is born, everything is taken care off before life started on our planet.

However scientists rule out the hand of super power, and they feel it is only by coincidence of favourable conditions by chance is responsible for the evolution of life. The debate will be endless unless scientists come out with convincing answers for the origin of the universe as well as origin of life. The power of the human brain is mainly responsible for the inquisitive nature of man to explore the environment and visible universe.

1.4 EVOLUTION OF HUMAN BRAIN

The evolutionary history of the human brain shows primarily a gradually bigger brain relative to body size during the evolutionary path from early primates to hominids and finally to *Homo sapiens*. Human brain size has been trending upwards since 2 million years ago, with a 3 factor increase. The primitive brains were little larger than chimpanzee brains. The increase has been seen as larger human brain volume as we progressed along the human timeline of evolution. The brain size increased from about 600 cm^3 to 1500 cm^3. This increase in brain size topped with Neanderthals; since then the average brain size has been a shrinking over the past 28,000 years. The male brain has decreased from 1,500 cm^3 to 1,350 cm^3 while the female brain has shrunk by the same relative proportion.

However it is argued that another essential element of brain evolution in humans is rearrangement. Larger brains require more wiring, but more wiring can become inefficient. The brain, therefore, became reorganized for efficiency. Furthermore the average body size of the Neanderthals was larger which lead to bigger brain size.

The brain, with about hundred billion neuron cells and 100 trillion connections is the most complex thing out of all creations. The brain is capable of controlling sugar in the blood, and body temperature to a great degree of precision which no man-made machine can perform. The brain weighs mere 1500 grams, and consists of convoluted mass of grey and white matter serving to control many of the bodily functions as efficiently as a pilot guides his aeroplane through a storm.

The brain operates on the same amount of power as 40-watt light bulb and the brain cells can hold five times the information stored in the Encyclopaedia Britannica. Yet it uses only 20% of the oxygen that enters the blood stream.

The brain is broadly divided into two hemispheres: The left hemisphere, and the right hemisphere, the left hemisphere is larger than the right hemisphere, and each hemisphere is responsible for specified brain functions.

The left hemisphere is responsible for verbal functions such as language, logic, mathematics, analytical ability, and critical thinking. The right brain is responsible for functions such as pattern recognition, face recognition, visual imagery, music, intuition and creativity. It is well established that majority of people make use of the left hemisphere while a small fraction is capable of utilising the right brain as well as the left brain. Those who can use both brains efficiently are geniuses.

The brain cortex can be classified into different lobes: Frontal lobe, Parietal lobe, Temporal lobe, Occipital lobe, and Cerebral Lobe. These are responsible for the processing of our sensations, how we perceive the world.

The Frontal Lobe (forehead) is responsible for motor control, complex thoughts, emotions, judgement and planning. This lobe gradually develops with age. This explains why children are not so good at planning.

The Temporal Lobes are located at the temple. They are responsible for timing and attention. These lobes mature by the age 7, and play an important part in memory as well as processing both auditory (hearing) and olfactory (smell) input.

The Parietal Lobes are the key for all our perceptions, and responsible for spatial and language functions. The left parietal lobe is responsible for language, while the right lobe is responsible for spatial function. This helps us to distinguish between big and small, and shape of objects.

The Occipital Lobe, located at the back of our head, is responsible for sight and processes all visual input. The Cerebral Lobes are the most sensitive brain structure. They are responsible for moving short term memory traces into long term memory traces. This region also helps to maintain homeostatic, attention and concentration.

1.5 BRAIN FUNCTION

A neuron or nerve cell is an electrically excitable cell that processes and transmits information through electrical and chemical signals. These signals travel from one neuron to another via synapses at a speed of approximately 300 kilometres per hour. Neurons can connect to each other to form neural networks.

The neurons are the main components of the two nervous systems. The Central Nervous System (CNS) comprises of the brain-spinal chord combination and its function is to control all bodily activities. The Peripheral Nervous System (PNS), on the other hand, consists of nerves and ganglia on the outside of the brain and spinal chord, and its main function is to facilitate communication from the brain to the limbs and organs.

A typical neuron possesses a cell body (soma), dendrites, and an axon. The term "neurite" is used to describe either a dendrite or an axon, particularly in its undifferentiated stage. Dendrites are thin structures that arise from the cell body, often extending for hundreds of micrometres and branching multiple times, giving rise to a complex "dendritic tree." An axon is a special cellular extension that arises from the cell body at a site called the axon hillock and travels for a distance, as far as 1 meter in humans or even more in other species.

The cell body of a neuron frequently gives rise to multiple dendrites, but never to more than one axon, although the axon may branch hundreds of times before it terminates. At the majority of synapses, signals are sent from the axon of one neuron to a dendrite of another. There are, however, many exceptions to these rules: neurons that lack dendrites, neurons that have no axon, synapses that connect an axon to another axon or a dendrite to another dendrite, etc.

A voltage gradient is maintained across the membrane due to ion concentration differences on either side. This voltage gradient pumps the ions, such as sodium, potassium and calcium, across the membrane, and will excite the neurons electrically. Thus, the electrochemical pulses travel along the cell's axons and activate synaptic connections with other cells.

Neurons of the brain do not undergo cell divisions like other cells in the body. Generally, some types of stem cells are involved in generating neurons. In humans, neurogenesis largely ceases during adulthood; but in two brain areas, the hippocampus and olfactory bulb, there is strong evidence for generation of substantial numbers of new neurons.

The brains filing system is more or less same in all human beings. The brain has two types of memory, Episodic and Semantic. The episodic memory is more specific in terms of space and time. It preserves the past events in our personal life. That is why we are able to remember who was sitting next to us during a flight journey to America five years ago. This memory might fade away with age. The semantic memory, on the other hand, is related to language, concepts, and learning skills. This memory does not decrease with age; it might even improve with age. For example, cycling we learnt in the childhood does not fade away even if were not cycling for decades.

1.6 HEART BRAIN

Few scientists exploring "intelligence" are reviving the cardio centric model of Aristotle. According to Dr. Mohamed Ghlian, the heart has a miniature brain that functions, sometimes, independent of the head-brain. According to this theory the intellect lies in the heart and not in the head brain. The new branch known as Neuroradiology is relatively new and making startling discoveries.

Our heart has its own nervous system that is composed of approximately 40,000 neurons called sensory neurites, and is more than a simple blood pumping device. The messages from the heart influence the activities of the brain such as perception, decision making, and other cognitive processes.

The heart has its own peculiar logic which can trigger or inhibit brain's electrical activity.

Thus, it was revealed that Heart has its own intrinsic nervous system that operates and processes information independently of the Brain. This is why it may be called as "little brain' of the heart, and because of this, Heart Transplants are made possible, since severed nerve connections do not reconnect in a different body. Another more fascinating observation made is the fact, even though brain and heart receive and respond to information about a future event even before the event actually happens, it is the heart that receives this intuitive information even before the Brain does. Heart affects mental clarity, creativity, emotional balance and the sensation of love. The magnetic field of the heart is estimated to be 500 times stronger than the magnetic field of the brain in our head.

In a study from 2002, researchers from the University of Arizona and University of Hawaii collaborated to publish a paper titled "Changes in Heart Transplant Recipients that Parallel the Personalities of their Donors." Ten recipients who received heart transplants underwent evaluation through a series of open-ended interviews. The patients who underwent heart transplant not only received heart from the donor but they experienced dramatic change in their behaviour, food habits and developed new skills such as showing love for music and playing musical instruments which they never knew.

There was a case of a meat eater overnight turned into vegetarian as he received heart from a vegetarian donor. Another case was of a young donor who was a violin musician that made the older classical-music-hating recipient all of a sudden want to listen to hours of it after surgery. A funny incident is about a 47-year-old man receiving the heart of a 14-year-old girl injured in a gymnastics accident. His wife commented at how he changed after surgery acting and thinking like a teenager. Understanding the nature of brain and mind is very important to know how we gain knowledge.

1.7 HOW THE BRAIN BECOMES MIND?

Now, let us try to define "mind." Not so easy. You may be surprised to find that there is no single, agreed upon definition of the mind. The psychiatric, mental health and medical professions each have their own functional definitions.

Our senses take in information from the environment. Since we are born, the five sensory organs receive information continuously. These become electrical signals, comprising of ions, which travel through the nervous system to the brain which, then, gives them meaning and responds by releasing neurochemicals and dispatching electrical signals which, in turn, regulate the body, control movement and influence emotions.

Depending on the nature of our existing emotions and thoughts, we exhibit our mood and behaviour. When you hit a metal object with another, a sound is produced. The metal objects are visible but not the sound. In a similar way, explains a neuroscientist, when a neuron carrying information meets another neuron, a thought is produced.

Whenever sensory information enters a neuron, it activates the previously created impressions or images, and this interaction produces "thoughts" in the form of electrochemical and electromagnetic signals. Thus past sensations become the ground for future thoughts and emotions. The new thoughts will then influence how we feel and behave. Thus thoughts are produced as a result of continuous and coordinated processes taking place. It may be noted that the objects and the brain are visible, not the thoughts. Thoughts are released because of sensory inputs into neurons which is a continuous phenomenon throughout our life.

Thus the "Mind" is the place or junction where sensory information is converted into thoughts and emotions. It is estimated that 73000 thoughts are produced before the mind takes rest during deep-sleep.

Mind is related to brain. Most people do not find any difference between the two words mind and brain. Most scientists and thinkers believe that the brain and the mind are one and cannot be separated. Most of the time, these two words are used interchangeably even though the brain is known to be a physical thing, mind is considered to be mental, non-materialistic.

The brain is composed of nerve cells and blood vessels whereas the mind is not like that. While the brain has a definite shape, the mind does not have one. We can see and touch the brain whereas it is not possible to do this with the mind.

As the brain is made up of several materials, it can be studied. On the other hand, it is hard to conduct studies on the mind as it is not made up of any material. The brain, which is the centre of the nervous system, coordinates the movements, thoughts and feelings. But these are felt through the mind. Thus mind refers to a person's understanding of things and also conscience. Mind refers to a person's thought process.

Spiritualists talk of mind as the set of cognitive faculties that involve the processes of thinking, decision making, storing and retrieving information and the body consciousness of identifying oneself as I, me and mine when dealing with the external world. Others, classify mind as conscious mind, subconscious mind and super conscious mind, etc.

1.8 MEMORY

The information about an event is registered somewhere in the neuron, which we call memory. Memory is like a computer hard disc. Over a period of time, the old impressions as well as the new impressions are stored at different places in the neurons. The information stored inside the memories is changed each time new information enters the neurons, the mind gets activated and the individual exhibits new feelings or emotions depending on the number of neurons or neural networks that are activated. Three types of sensory memories have been identified, Iconic, Echoic, and Haptic depending on the type of stimuli such as visual, or touch. However, brain memory can be broadly classified into short-term and long-term.

Short-term memory is believed to rely mostly on an acoustic code for storing information, and to a lesser extent a visual code. While short-term memory encodes information acoustically, long-term memory encodes it semantically.

The storage in sensory memory and short-term memory generally has a strictly limited capacity and duration, which means that information is not retained indefinitely. By contrast, long-term memory can store much larger quantities of information for potentially unlimited duration (sometimes a whole life span). Its capacity is immeasurably large. For example, given a random ten-digit mobile phone number we may remember it for only a few seconds before forgetting, suggesting it was stored in our short-term memory. On the other hand, we can remember telephone numbers for many years through repetition; this information is said to be stored in long-term memory.

Short-term memory pertains to the areas in the frontal lobe and parietal lobe. Long-term memory, on the other hand, is maintained by more stable and permanent changes in neural connections widely spread throughout the brain. The hippocampus is essential (for learning new information) to the consolidation of information from short-term to long-term memory. For example, after removal of both his hippocampi a patient does not seem to store information itself and there will be only a short attention span. Also changes have been observed in the neural connections. Research has suggested that long-term memory storage in humans may be maintained by DNA

We have heard of only a few gigabytes of storage space in computers or other storage devices. In the brain, neurons combine so that each one helps with many memories at a time, exponentially increasing the brain's memory storage capacity to around few million gigabytes.

1.9 BRAIN AND CONSCIOUSNESS

There are two fundamental issues that bothered both the eastern and western philosophers even before science originated. These are:

What emerged first, consciousness or matter, and whether the world is knowable? This so called mind-body problem is very much alive and lot of research is being done by modern scientists. Earlier it was thought consciousness was the subject matter of only philosophers.

It is necessary, before understanding the nature of consciousness, to draw a clear distinction between the two worlds: The physical world and the mental world. The physical world is perceived through the five sensory organs and is accessible for observation by others. The mental world, on the contrary, is populated, not by material objects but by thoughts. Thoughts, obviously, not located in space-time but seem to occupy world of their own, a private universe of the individual and is not accessible to others. This is the reason we hear "My thought," "My conscience" and "My dream," etc. Thoughts of two persons might be different even though both are located at the same point in space-time.

Also, these thoughts that pervade the mind are found to be spontaneous, irrelevant, unconnected and illogical; these are yet to be addressed by researchers.

Our mental and physical worlds are not two independent isolated worlds, but both are coupled to one another. Our mental activity comprises of processing a constant stream of information, which is stored in our memory and proceeds to generate new activity either by stimulating the appearances of new thoughts or re-shaping the existing ones. There are two main theories appearing recently trying to explain how consciousness is different from matter: The Electromagnetic theories and The Quantum Brain theories. In general, however, quantum mind theories other than these Quantum Brain Dynamics (QBD) approaches do not treat consciousness as an electromagnetic phenomenon.

One theory proposed by nuero-biologists McFadden and Pockett, relates to electromagnetic theory. The starting assumption for their theory is that whenever a neuron fires, it generates an action potential in the next neuron down the line. It also generates disturbance in the electromagnetic field that surrounds the next neuron in the line. They proposed that the brain's electromagnetic field creates a representation of the information in the neurons. Studies undertaken towards the end of the 20th century have shown that conscious experience correlates not with the number of neurons firing, but with the synchrony of that firing. The synchronous firing of neurons is, in this theory, supposed to amplify the influence of the brain's EM field fluctuations to a much greater extent than would be possible with the unsynchronized firing of neurons. The digital information from neurons is integrated to form a conscious electromagnetic information (cemi) field in the brain. Therefore, consciousness is suggested to be the component of this field that is transmitted back to neurons, and communicates its state externally. Thoughts are viewed as electromagnetic representations of neuronal information, and the experience of 'free-will' in our choice of actions is argued to be our subjective experience of the *cemi* field acting on our neurons.

There is another theory, known as Quantum Brain Dynamics, is in a way another form of electromagnetic theory. This theory proposes that the interaction between the energy quanta of the quantum field and the bimolecular waves of the neuronal network produces consciousness. However, another theorist proposes that the quantum states produce two poles, a subjective representation of the external world and also the internal self.

There is, yet, another theory of consciousness based on Sting theory. According to this, thoughts and emotions can be considered as energy in theoretical terms. Most often, they occur as a result of the stimuli experienced. Stimuli pass through sensory memory and are carried by the nervous system to the brain, where associations are made between short-term and long-term memory, thereby passing through various environmental and genetic filters before manifesting as a behavioural response that can be superficially studied in terms of interpersonal communication.

Sarfatti, another neuroscientist, proposed a consciousness theory that is based on the postulation which can be found in the superstring theory of physics. This theory is based on the fact that the most fundamental particles of matter - for instance, protons, electrons and neutrons - are composed of infinitesimally small vibrating strings which combine with other strings of similar resonance. In this case, infinitesimally small would be about 100 billion times smaller than a proton. Analogous to the strings on a musical instrument such as the violin or cello, they vibrate at various frequencies, allowing for combination and re-combination of resonant strings in order to form the particles of matter with which we are familiar that form the molecules which, in turn, form the 'solid' physical world we experience with our senses.

Therefore, consciousness is essentially composed of miniscule resonating strings that create an electromagnetic field that resonates at a particular frequency. The human body is indeed an aerial that can transmit and receive energy. Thoughts and their concomitant energy do have an outlet by means of visible emotional expressions and the radiation of an electromagnetic (EM) field. With this groundwork laid, it is now possible to postulate how these concepts tie in with interpersonal communication.

Another neurobiologists, Bernard Baars, states that "no serious researcher, I know, believes in an electromagnetic theory of consciousness and it is not really worth talking about it scientifically."

1.10 HYPNOSIS

Hypnosis is the induction of a state of consciousness in which a person apparently loses the power of voluntary action and is highly responsive to suggestion or direction by the hypnotist. Its use in therapy, typically to recover suppressed memories or to allow modification of behaviour, has been revived but is still controversial.

During hypnosis, a person is said to have heightened focus and concentration. The person can concentrate intensely on a specific thought or memory, while blocking out sources of distraction. Hypnotised subjects are said to show an increased response to suggestions. Hypnosis is usually induced by a procedure known as a hypnotic induction involving a series of preliminary instructions. The hypnotized individual appears to heed only to the communications of the hypnotist. He seems to respond in an uncritical, automatic fashion, ignoring all aspects of the environment other than those pointed out to him by the hypnotist. He sees, feels, smells, and otherwise perceives in accordance with the hypnotist's suggestions, even though these suggestions may be in apparent contradiction to the stimuli that impinge upon him. Even the subject's memory and awareness of self may be altered to the extent they are reflected into the subject's subsequent waking activity.

Hypnotherapy

Hypnotherapy makes use of hypnosis in psychotherapy. It is used by licensed physicians and psychologists. They use hypnosis to treat depression, anxiety, eating disorders, sleep disorders, compulsive gaming, and posttraumatic stress. Some certified hypnotherapists who are not physicians or psychologists often treat smoking and weight management. Modern hypnotherapy has been used in a variety of forms with varying success.

Self-hypnosis

Self-hypnosis happens when a person hypnotises oneself, commonly involving the use of self-imposed thoughts known as 'auto-suggestion.' The technique is often used to increase motivation for a diet, quit smoking or reduce stress. People who practice self-hypnosis sometimes require assistance; some people use devices known as mind machines to assist in the process, whereas others use hypnotic recordings.

Self-hypnosis is claimed to help with stage fright, relaxation, and physical well-being. Hypnosis is not a unitary state and therefore should show different patterns of EEG activity depending upon the task being experienced. A review of available literature has shown that enhanced *theta* state is observed during hypnosis when there is task performance or concentrative hypnosis, but not when the highly hypnotizable individuals are passively relaxed, somewhat sleepy and/or more diffuse in their attention.

Hypno-surgery

It is the term given to an operation, where the patient is sedated using hypnotherapy rather than anaesthetics. It is still in experimental stage, and not often used. During hypno-surgery, hypnotherapists help the patient to control his subconscious reflexes so that he does not feel pain. They might feel tingling or tickling sensation instead.

1.11 PAST LIFE REGRESSION

Past life regression is a technique that uses hypnosis to recover what practitioners believe are memories of past lives or incarnations, though others regard them as fantasies or delusions or a type of confabulation. Past life regression is typically undertaken either in pursuit of a spiritual experience, or in a psychotherapeutic setting. Most advocates loosely adhere to beliefs about reincarnation, though religious traditions that incorporate reincarnation generally do not include the idea of repressed memories of past lives.

In ancient Indian literature, especially, the Patanjali's Yoga Sutra mentions about past life regression concept in detail. Written during the 2nd century BC, the Hindu scholar Patañjali discussed the idea of the soul becoming burdened with an accumulation of impressions of the karmas from previous births. Patañjali called the process of past-life regression *prati-prasav*, and saw that it addresses current problems through memories of past lives.

In 1988, Brian Weiss, an American psychiatrist, started using past-life regression technique for treating patients using hypnosis. Later he published, best-selling book, *Many Lives, Many Masters.* The technique he used during past life regression involves making the subject answering a series of questions while being hypnotized to reveal identity and events during his past lives He is treating patients of their current problems linking to the events in one of their past lives.

The patients undergoing the past life regression must have two beliefs: faith in reincarnation and suggestions by the hypnotist regarding the contents of memories reported.

The memories are experienced as vivid as those based on events experienced in one's life, impossible to differentiate from true memories of actual events, and accordingly any damage, that results, can be difficult to undo. Past life regression (PLR) is a highly controversial subject in the field of therapy.

1.12 TELEPATHY

The origin of the concept of telepathy in the Western civilization can be tracked to the late 19th century. Scientists were able to apply advanced concepts to study brain and mental activity with the hope that it would help, one day, to understand paranormal phenomena. The modern concept of telepathy emerged in this context.

Telepathy is also known as thought (mind) reading, thought intervention and thought removal. In the late 19th century the magician by name Irving Bishop of Washington conducted thought-reading demonstrations on stage.

Another famous thought reader was the magician Stuart Cumberland. He was famous for performing blindfolded feats such as identifying a hidden object in a room that a person had picked out or asking someone to imagine a murder scene and then attempt to read the subject's thoughts and identify the victim and re-enact the crime.

It was established, after cross examination by scientists, the performers in the above feats, are using the help of a subject or signal codes from a subject without the knowledge of the audience.

1.13 TELEKINESIS

Telekinesis is the ability to move or bend objects without physical contact. Some people think that the magnetic waves coming out of the brain can move objects or even bend them. Also it was noticed some persons are able to attract metal objects like knives which stick on to their body. It is presumed the magnetic field of some people is much stronger than majority, and so such feats are possible. No scientific basis has been established yet.

1.14 BRAIN – COMPUTER INTERFACE (BCI)

Brain-computer interface systems, although still in developmental and experimental stages, are becoming increasingly more powerful and applicable. Advancements in neural signalling research make it one of the hottest fields in biomedical engineering.

Earlier this year, researchers indeed trained four people suffering epilepsy to move a computer cursor with the power of thought. The patients, who were waiting to have brain surgery, were already fitted with small sheets of signal-detecting electrodes on the surfaces of their brains.

The patients were asked to perform certain tasks - such as opening and closing their hands and sticking out their tongue - while scientists determined what brain signals were associated with these movements. Next, the signals from these movements were matched up with movements of the cursor on the screen. For example, the thought of opening of the right hand might move the cursor to the right. The subjects were then asked to move the cursor from one spot to another on the screen by thinking about making the movements.

The patients had some difficulty at first, but each was able to control the cursor with their thoughts and with over 70 percent accuracy after a few minutes of practice. One patient was operating at 100 percent accuracy by the end of the trial as reported by Daniel Moran of Washington University.

Brown University and Cyber kinetics Terotechnology Systems, Inc., is working to develop a system called Brain Gate. Here a sensor is implanted on the surface of the primary motor cortex, the area of the brain responsible for movement. The sensor, smaller than a penny, has hair-thin electrode probes that penetrate about a millimetre into the brain and are designed to pick up electrical impulses from the motor neurons.

The goal of study and its follow-ups is to develop a safe, effective, and unobtrusive universal system for physically disabled people to control a wide array of devices, such as computers, wheelchairs and robotic arms with their thoughts.

1.15 BRAIN-COMPUTER - BRAIN INTERFACE (BCBI)

International researchers are reporting that they have built the first brain- to computer- to again brain, interface that allows two humans, separated by the internet, to consciously communicate with each other, with no additional sensory cues. One researcher, attached to a brain-computer interface (BCI) in India, successfully sent words into the brain of another researcher in France, who was wearing a computer-to-brain interface (CBI). In short, the researchers have created a device that enables *telepathy*. Over the last few years, researchers have started to get quite good at reading your brain activity or your thoughts.

The researchers are using different techniques. On the BCI side, they used a fairly standard EEG, while for the CBI, which requires a more involved setup, a trans- cranial magnetic stimulation (TMS) rig was used. Few commercial units are now available, and more are being planned.

Scientists have used a direct brain-to-brain connection to enable two participants, almost 1.5 km apart, played a question-answer type game by transmitting signals from one brain to the other via internet. This is the recent achievement by an Assistant Professor of psychology, Andrea Stocco, at the University of Washington. The participants wear a cap with about 96 electrodes and connected to ECG machine that records his brain activity. The experiment was repeated with different pairs of participants, and claimed successful communication. The sessions were a random mix of 10 real games and 10 control games that were structured in the same manner. This experiment, as it is claimed, is the first to link two brains, so that one person can guess what is in the other man's mind.

1.16 ARTIFICIAL INTELLIGENCE

Artificial intelligence (AI) is the intelligence exhibited by a machine or a software. The central problem or goal of research in this field of study include reasoning, knowledge, planning, natural language processing, communication, perception, learning and the ability to move and manipulate objects. The goal of Scientists, in short, is to create a machine that can accomplish the functions what the human brain do. The scientists are using in AI, a large number of tools like mathematical optimisation, logic, probability, linguistics, psychology and neuroscience.

Aeroplanes, rockets, missiles, and spacecraft, all use one form of AI or the other. They carry on-board computers for processing data to follow precise flight path using navigation, guidance and control systems. Recently, driverless car has been developed and being tested on roads. For flight safety, the pilot has to monitor number of panels at close intervals, and the strain it causes is one of the reasons for accidents. At places where fire or nuclear radiation hazards exist, deploying robots with AI is conceivable.

However, scientists are aiming to create AI to excel that of human brain. Whether it is possible or not in the near future, many are raising objections on ethical grounds. When AI matches or exceeds that of human brain, it is called 'singularity' by AI researches. Physicist, John von Neumann, was the person who coined the word singularity in AI. The singularity in AI is a hypothesis where a robot would become capable of building another robot that is more intelligent than itself. When this process is repeated we end up creating a robot whose intelligence exceeds that of a human being.

But what happens when machine intelligence supersedes the intelligence of its creator, the consequences will be immense and will become a threat to our existence. But it is unlikely that a machine will have a creative power that matches human mind and its intuitive knowledge.

1.17 BRAIN WAVES

Our thoughts, emotions and behaviours is the result of communication between neurons within our brains. Brainwaves are produced by synchronised electrical pulses from masses of neurons communicating with each other.

Brainwaves are detected using sensors placed on the scalp. They are divided into bandwidths to describe their functions, and are best thought of as a continuous spectrum of consciousness; The low frequency waves are named as "Delta" while the high frequency waves are known as "Gamma."

Our brainwaves change according to what we are doing and feeling. When slower brainwaves are dominant we can feel tired, slow, sluggish, or dreamy. The higher frequencies are dominant when we feel wired, or hyper-alert.

When a person is focusing attention on something, the brain emits waves. This activity comprises of firing of thousands of neurons simultaneously generating wave at the same frequency that ranges from 10 to 100Hz. Brainwave frequencies are so widely different, they don't interfere with radio waves. Even if that was the case, brain waves are so weak, they are hardly measurable at all.

Our brainwave profile and our daily experience of the world are inseparable. When our brainwaves are out of balance, there will be corresponding problems in our emotional or neuro-physical health. Research has identified brainwave patterns associated with all sorts of emotional and neurological conditions. Instabilities in brain rhythms correlate with aggressive behaviour, migraines, epilepsy, sleep apnoea, vertigo, etc.

Brainwave frequency is measured in Hertz (cycles per second) and they are divided into bands as explained below:

The MIT, has installed MEG based instruments to measure brain waves. The MEG scanner consists of a helmet that contains 306 sensors spaced uniformly across its surface. These superconducting quantum interference detectors (SQUID) are cooled to near absolute zero, which makes them superconductive and, able to measure even the slightest magnetic signals from the brain.

Delta Waves (0.5–3Hz): These brainwaves are the slowest but loudest brainwaves (low frequency and deeply penetrating, like a drum beat). They are generated in deepest meditation and dreamless sleep.

Theta Waves (3–8 Hz): Theta brainwaves occur most often in sleep but are also dominant in the deep meditation. It acts as our gateway to learning and memory. In theta, our senses are withdrawn from the external world and focused on signals originating from within. In theta we are in a dream; vivid imagery, intuition and information beyond our normal conscious awareness. It's where we hold our 'stuff', our fears, troubled history, and nightmares.

Alpha Waves (8–12 Hz): Alpha brainwaves are dominant during quietly flowing thoughts, and in some meditative states. Alpha is 'the power of now', being here, in the present. Alpha is the resting state for the brain. Alpha waves aid overall mental coordination, calmness, alertness, mind/body integration and learning.

Beta Waves (12–38 Hz): Beta brainwaves dominate our normal waking state of consciousness when attention is directed towards cognitive tasks and the outside world. Beta is a 'fast' activity, present when we are alert, attentive, engaged in problem solving, judgment, decision making.

Gamma Waves (38–42 Hz): Gamma brainwaves are the fastest of brain waves (high frequency, like a flute), and relate to simultaneous processing of information from different brain areas. It passes information rapidly, and as the most subtle of the brainwave frequencies, the mind has to be quiet to access it. Gamma was traditionally dismissed as 'spare brain noise' until researchers discovered it was highly active when in states of universal love, altruism, and the 'higher virtues'. Gamma rhythms modulate perception and consciousness, disappearing under anaesthesia. Gamma is also above the frequency of neuronal firing, so how it is generated remains a mystery. The presence of Gamma relates to expanded consciousness and spiritual emergence.

It is understood that a process that changes your perception might also change your brainwaves. Chemical interventions such as medications or recreational drugs are the most common methods to alter brain function; however brainwave training is also very effective.

Our knowledge configures our brain, our brain configures our genes, and our genes configure our behaviour. Practicing over the long term, traditional eastern methods (such as meditation and yoga) might train our brainwaves into balance.

1.18 RECENT ADVANCES

Neuroscientists have succeeded as how to manipulate lab animal's brain circuitry to turn on or off a particular behaviour of the animal. They hope to find solutions to people suffering from neurological disorders in future. This was done under U.S. President Obama's initiative on brain research.

Another research project that is initiated recently is DREADS, known as Designer Receptors Exclusively Activated by Designer Drugs. Here, the brain neurons are genetically engineered to produce desired behaviour in mice, says, Bryan Roth of North Carolina University, USA. By injecting a particular molecule can make mice to ignore a bowl of food or make them feast at the will of the scientist by injecting another type of molecule. New York Times quotes on 11 July 2014, after a neuroscience conference on 'Brain Science', 'we do not know as much as we think we do. Are we ever going to figure out how the brain works?'

After decades of research, diseases like Schizophrenia and Alzheimer's still do not find treatment. Despite countless investigations into serotonin and other neurotransmitters, there is still no method to cure clinical depression. And for all the excitement about brain-imaging techniques, the limitations of fMRI studies are, as evidenced by different authors in different books. In spite of the many remarkable advances in neuroscience, despite the initiation of $1.6 billion Human Brain Project of Europe and $300 million Brain Initiative Project of America. Many scientists feel some path-breaking theories must evolve to understand the working of the brain. The ten questions presented below have no answers from scientists as on today. This shows that what is understood about brain-functioning is less than ten percent.

1. What is consciousness?
2. Why thoughts are spontaneous, unconnected, irrelevant and illogical?
3. Why and how do we sleep and dream?
4. How do we store and access memory?
5. How a creative idea is generated?
6. What is free will, do we have free will?
7. How does one feel depression, pain and pleasure?
8. How precise movement and reaction, say, during martial arts, possible.
9. How the opinions are formed, and decision among choices?
10. To what extent, our personality and behaviour are determined by brain and genes.

2

SCIENCE AND TECHNOLOGY

Even though scientific thoughts are more than four centuries old, people at large realised its importance only from the days of the Industrial Revolution. Western society was driven by an unshakable faith in the power of science and technology.

People realised the impact of technology when they saw the Steam engines are moving on railroads, electric lights in the streets and airplanes flying, the telegraph that enabled distance communication, typewriter, motion pictures for entertainment and use of light weight plastics. These were just some of the significant inventions during this unique moment in history, when man thought he would be able to control the environment around him and to improve his living conditions beyond limits.

One of the main driving forces for the rapid progress in science and technology is the agricultural revolution. One person working in the field was able to produce food to feed 50 to 100 people depending on the degree of innovations employed in different countries. This had resulted in population of idle people to look for alternate occupations.

From the beginning of the 20th century, technology itself was transformed from a haphazard process of invention to a science-based discipline. This made progress merely a matter of well-directed effort.

The influence of modern technology was felt even in rural areas through agricultural innovations, the spread of newspapers and the construction of railroads and highways passing through the villages. The desire to participate in this new world inspired many people to migrate to cities, where many new technologies were tackling urgent problems of housing, food supply, hygiene, sewage, traffic mobility, crime control and communication.

The revolutions in science and technology also contributed to the change in social perception and values. Computers and machine tools came into existence and contributed to precision and uniformity. This has set in the industrial culture with a concept of manager-worker to achieve desired production goals. This has resulted in a sort of mechanised life in the society.

Science and technology created a new economy, different from agricultural economy, and the man is driven too much towards comfortable materialistic life. It is interesting to look into what goals are set for science and technology.

2.1 THE GOAL OF SCIENCE

The word "physics" originated from Greek, means Nature. The word "science" came from Latin and means "to know." The organised attempt of man to know about his surrounding environment and the resultant knowledge he acquired became known as "science." Man has always been curious about the world, especially about the phenomena such as repetition of day and night, of the seasons, and of the movement of the planets around the sun.

The natural instinct of man to seek and to find the causes for the phenomenal world has driven him to search for ways and means of observation, reasoning, model making, experimentation and predictions. This has resulted in discovery of theories and physical laws. Many a times these theories failed to explain discrepancies. This resulted in modifications to the existing theory or discovering an alternate theory.

This process continues even today. For example, the three laws discovered by Newton became so important, even today, engineers are applying them for designing bridges and rockets. Albert Einstein, few hundred years later, pointed out the limitations of application of Newt's laws. The basic flaw in Newton's laws is the fact that he assumed a static universe in which time flows uniformly. Secondly, as the speed of the object increases Newton's laws are not applicable. Again, at the subatomic level, these laws are not valid. Lastly, the claim that the Newton's laws can be used to predict the future course of a moving object, its position and velocity, was proved wrong. Finally it was established that Newton's laws are not deterministic. It is not possible to predict the weather, occurrences of earth quakes or volcanoes.

Science has witnessed discovery of new theories in almost every discipline: evolutionary theories, thermodynamics theory, Einstein's relativity and gravitational theories, big bang theory, quantum electrodynamics, quantum chromo dynamics, unified theories like super gravity, super symmetry, string theory, Theory of Every Thing, Plate Tectonic theory, black hole theory, information theory and chaos theory etc.

Scientists noticed that they have to apply different laws and theories to explain different phenomena taking place in different parts of the universe. This is not tenable in the long run. They observed that there are basically four forces that are operating and controlling nature; these account for majority of the phenomena taking place. These are: Gravitational force, Electromagnetic force, the weak force, and the strong force; these are known as the four fundamental forces of nature. For example, the gravitational force is behind the planetary motion, formation of stars and galaxies, and the structure of the present universe. The electromagnetic force is responsible for magnetic, optical, crystal, chemical and life phenomena. The weak force is responsible for radioactivity and finally the strong force is behind phenomena like nuclear fission and fusion.

If one wants to know the working of our universe, scientists have to come up with a single Super force, (Fig. 2.1) that can explain the origin of the universe as well as the subatomic processes. Therefore, all the four forces mentioned supposed to have originated from this Super Force. So the main goal of scientists around the world is to find the origin of the universe, life and consciousness.

To achieve this goal scientists have been trying to combine the four forces of nature into a single super force. They have been devising theories like super gravity, super symmetry, theory of everything etc. However they are facing insurmountable problems, since one theory is not fitting into another theory. One of the main problems they are facing is how to combine the Einstein's gravitational theory with that of Quantum mechanical theories.

2.2 WHAT ARE PROBLEMS FACING SCIENTISTS

It is time to juxtapose all the scientific theories in order to gauge scientific progress during the last four hundred years.

Classical mechanics, today, arrived at the important conclusion that the classical determinism, as envisaged by Newton, is dead. Global reality, the cosmos as a whole, from the subatomic particles to the accelerating universe is out of reach. Scientists can only isolate subsystems for study, and set up experimental screens on which to project this inaccessible whole. In theory, if one were to make any predictions about the future, it would be necessary to have a complete and detailed knowledge of the state of the universe.

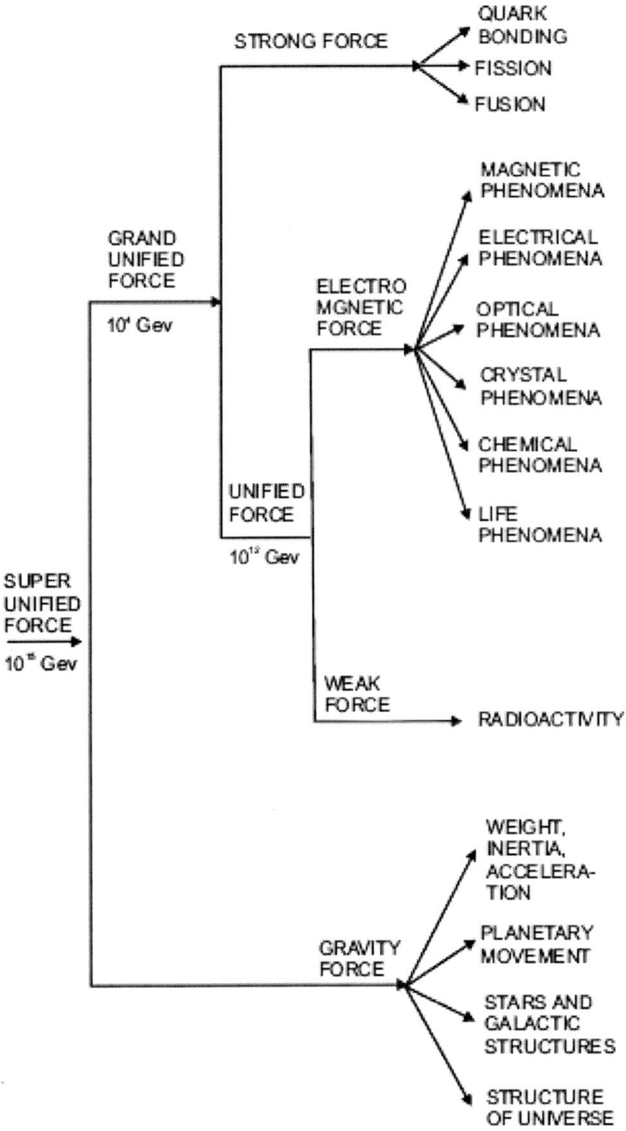

Fig. 2.1 Goal of Science

From the second law of thermodynamics, what we learnt is the fact that a given system has a natural tendency to move from order to disorder, increasing entropy in the process. Boltzmann attempted to save the situation by reducing the second law of thermodynamics to a mere statement of probability. However, his statistical model, which assumed that all particles or molecules behave identically like solid balls, proved futile. As a result Fermi–Dirac statistics has to be invented to explain the behaviour of electrons in a semiconductor. Again to explain the bizarre behaviour of electrons at super cooled conditions, Bose-Einstein statistical model has been evolved. The major problem encountered in Thermodynamics is the fact that most processes are irreversible in nature, and a new physics to understand them is yet to be evolved.

Darwin, while formulating his theory of evolution, grossly underestimated the influence of environment on the evolutionary processes. The origin of life, still remains a mystery. His theory could not explain how consciousness evolved. All living beings are dissipative structures, and will survive as long as energy is supplied from the environment. But organized activity in a closed system invariably decays in accordance with the second law of thermodynamics. It is paradoxical that in a universe, apparently dying under the influence of second law, but in the same universe, the biological systems are evolving with increasing levels of complexity.

This fact has been highlighted by David C Pack, the author of the book "Does God Exist" published in August 2014. According to the First Law of Thermodynamics, matter and energy can be neither created nor destroyed. Therefore, all who state that the universe came into existence from *nothing* violates this law. Further he compares the Second Law of

Thermodynamics and says he found proof of God's existence based on his science knowledge. Till then he has known God only as a matter of faith. He says careful examination of scientific theories will demonstrate that an all-powerful Supreme Being, of infinite intelligence, carefully provided more than sufficient proof to remove all doubt that He exists. The author analyses the contradictions in different scientific theories: There are no natural processes that can alter either matter or energy in this way. This means that there is no *new* matter or energy coming into existence and there is no *new* matter or energy passing out of existence. All who state that the universe came into existence from *nothing* violate the first law of thermodynamics.

According to the Second Law of Thermodynamics, the universe is winding down—moving toward *disorder* with increasing entropy—not winding up or moving toward more perfect order and structure. In short, *the entire universe is winding down.* Even evolutionists admit that the theory of evolution and the second law of thermodynamics are completely incompatible with each other. It would hardly be possible to conceive of any two completely opposite principles than this principle of entropy increase and the principle of evolution.

Einstein, through his theories, special and general theories of relativity, introduced more confusion about the concepts of space, time and matter than they could explain. We run into difficulties when we try to comprehend the concept of empty space in which the constancy of speed of light has been defined. Empty space devoid of fields has lost its significance. The gravitational force between two bodies, the action at a distance, is not satisfactorily explained. The particle 'Graviton' is yet to be discovered. The major problem with Einstein's theories is the fact that they are not consistent with quantum mechanical theories and many other unified theories. Gravitation was dismissed as irrelevant to particle physics.

In the quantum mechanical theories, the particle-wave duality is not effectively comprehended. Quantum mechanics has its own probability theory, its own logic, and interpretations. In a way, it is totally isolated from the main stream science.

Mathematical problems, represented by a set of differential equations, and seeking solutions through integration is no more relevant and possible to understand chaotic systems. The whole seems to be more than the sum of its parts. The main problem, in mathematics, seems to be that mathematical language is no more adequate to explain the quantitative features of newly emerging theories such a Super- String theory, Chaos theory, and Unified theories where more than three spatial dimensions are involved. Scientists are facing two problems in working for the unified theories: *the mathematical representation of the new physical theory, and physical interpretation of the mathematical equations.*

All scientists are working in narrower and narrower fields, they often lose sight of "Totality." Science obviously cannot exist in bits and pieces and each claiming itself representing true science. We cannot apply different theories to explain different phenomena in different parts of the universe. This is why the goal of science is to unify all the four forces that control various phenomena in nature and arrive at a single super force. This single force must be able to explain everything in this universe, right from the inner working of atoms up to the cosmos. This force also must be able to explain the origin of the universe, life and consciousness.

When we juxtapose all the fundamental scientific theories-classical mechanics, thermodynamics, evolutionary theories, relativity theories, electrodynamics, quantum mechanical, quantum electrodynamics, grand unified theories, information and chaos theory- we can observe their closed nature with inherent limitations of one kind or other with no hope of unification and experimental verification as demanded by philosophers of science.

For a complex system like our universe, the whole is more than the sum of its individual components. Therefore studying part by part may not lead to complete knowledge of our universe. Furthermore, trying to predict the form and behaviour of a complex system like our universe, by the scientists, while working within the universe might be a self-defeating task. The discoveries, in astronomy and cosmology, such as accelerating universe, dark energy and dark matter, in recent times, stands as a proof. We know only the visible universe that constitutes less than five percent of total universe. What is happening at this instant in a distant galaxy like Andromeda is beyond human comprehension.

Biological systems also seem to be as complex as our universe. Unless scientists understand fully the human genome and the three-dimensional structure of protein as how it folds and unfolds, understanding the organisms will not be complete. Therefore, scientific theories have become closed theories, and can never provide a complete and definite description of reality.

In neurosciences too, consciousness is the greatest, most troubling mystery. The mind-body problem remains a perennial task to resolve. The link between genes and neuron connections in the brain to determine the human behaviour is incomplete. Any treatment for physical and mental illnesses based on trial and error, without complete knowledge might result in harmful side effects in the long run. How consciousness evolved from matter is beyond comprehension by scientists.

Let us say, a person, reading a book, hears a loud noise coming from the road through the window. The brain, after receiving the information through the ear provokes a thought. However, it is difficult to predict the action of the person that follows the triggering of thought wave in his mind. That is whether the person continues reading his book or closes the book and goes to the window to look at the source of the noise is difficult to predict. This conscious decision is prerogative of the individual. In other words consciousness is a function of the subject, not of brain.

Finally, scientist's assumption that consciousness evolved from matter, by the interactions of neurons, synapses, and number of firings in the brain, may be questionable.

The statements made by leading scientists have surprised many. The Consciousness has been defined as intuitively perceived knowledge of something in one's inner self. Many fall into the trap of equating consciousness with self-consciousness—to be conscious it is only necessary to be aware of the external world. Consciousness is a fascinating but elusive phenomenon: it is impossible to specify what it is, what it does, or why it has evolved. The term is impossible to define except in terms that are unintelligible without a grasp of what consciousness means.

The mind passes through three conscious states: the waking state (where mind perceives the external world); the dream state (where the mind becomes a projector) and the deep-sleep state (where the mind is absent). There seems to be a continuity of consciousness; otherwise we cannot continue our work today from where we left yesterday. This makes us feel that consciousness is a continuous stream without any break, even though, the consciousness appears to be broken or separated during dream state and deep-sleep state.

Therefore, consciousness is eternal and supreme and matter must have evolved from it. The more scientists are probing into the structure of the atom, they are discovering more and more new particles without an end. So far, more than 200 subatomic particles were discovered. Similarly, their probe into deep cosmos to understand its structure, more unknown things like dark matter and dark energy are being revealed. All this might point to one thing; the conscious probing by scientists might be creating new matter or energy. We may conclude that mind and consciousness is beyond the scope present science.

What discovery has baffled the greatest scientific minds of the past century, and why has it caused them to rethink the origin of our universe? New, and more powerful, telescopes have revealed mysteries about our universe that have raised new questions about the origin of life.

One cosmologist put it this way: "Many scientists, when they admit their views, incline toward the teleological or design argument. Surprisingly, most of the scientists who are talking about God, today, have no religious belief whatsoever in the past."

So, what are these stunning discoveries that have scientists suddenly speaking of God? Three revolutionary discoveries from the fields of astronomy and molecular biology stand out:

1. The universe had a beginning, and is facing a slow death.
2. The universe is just right for life to exist.
3. DNA coding reveals intelligence.

Scientists who imagine that the universe came into existence by accident, and through a series of coincidences, and life and consciousness evolved from inert matter, might have to change their thinking.

2.3 WHAT ARE THE GOALS OF TECHNOLOGY

While the goal of pure science is to know the origin of the universe and life, for technologists, there seems to be no clear goal. Scientists are understanding slowly that the human activity, through the application of technologies, is causing enormous problems for the flora and fauna on this planet. They are causing global warming, climate change and disturbing the delicate ecological balance of our biosphere, threatening the survival of our future generations.

What we need on this planet, to survive, are atmospheric air to breath, water to drink and food to eat. These are the primary requirements for our survival, and are made available to us by Mother Nature. We do not need engineers and scientists for providing these basic necessities. For life to exist on this planet, so many conditions, which are beyond the scope of scientists and engineers, must have been satisfied. For example, if the Earth were closer to the Sun by mere two percent the surface temperature will be so high that life cannot exist. Similarly, if the earth is away from the Sun a little, the cold conditions might not have allowed life to exist. If the mass of earth is little more or its radius is little less, the gravitational attraction would be large and life threatening gases like hydrogen, helium, organ etc. would have remained as part of our atmosphere, and life could not have evolved. Similarly, if the gravity of earth is little less, the atmosphere itself would not have existed to support life. The earth rotates on its own axis and tilted to one side. But for this, there would not have been day and night variations and change of seasons which are again essential for the life of plants and humans. The formation of ozone, from oxygen, in our atmosphere is another essential feature for life as it is protecting us from the harmful ultraviolet radiation from the sun.

We all know that the Sun is the only source of energy for all living beings on earth. Only a star that has a specific mass and radius, like our Sun, can have maximum life of 9 billion years. All other stars which have either less mass or more mass compared to the Sun, they cannot live long to make energy available to support life. This long life of our Sun is attributed to the delicate balance between its gravity that tries to compress and the thermal pressure generated, due to nuclear fusion reactions that try to expand.

The right atmosphere, the water, and the plants are there on our planet before human beings evolved. Just like milk is made ready in mother's breast before the child is born, air, water and food are taken care by Mother Nature. Some scientists do claim they brought green revolution by inventing fertilisers and insecticides. We all know the damage caused by these chemicals to the soil and our health. Today people are ready to pay double the price for products grown with natural fertilizers.

Life exists on our planet due to continual inflow of energy from the Sun. This energy, propels exchange of matter (biomass) with the dead, and exchange of information from the surroundings (both living and non-living). Without death of species new life cannot exist. No waste matter accumulates in the environment, and everything is recycled by natural processes. These are the findings of environmentalists and ecologists.

We can say, the only purpose of developing various technologies are to provide comforts to the physical body of human beings and not for basic survival needs. There seems to be no end for comforts man is seeking. This is attributable to the greed in man; he wants not only a shelter, he wants heating and cooling facilities, twenty four hours, during winter and summer seasons. He wants transportation facilities which can take him faster and faster from one place to other. He wants faster communications wherever he is. He wants education facilities for technology up gradation only to spoil the environment further.

Long back, Einstein quoted saying, "more and more technology development means less and less work needed by man towards the society; this must leave him free time which he can utilise for personality development, and his spiritual progress."

What we observe today is quiet contrary to what Einstein expected. The greed in man propelling him to involve in more and more technologies, but the free time as envisaged by Einstein for personality development of man is not in sight.

The scientists are now understanding the importance of protecting our environment and ecology. Environmentalists, for the last few decades, have been continually warning us, but the various governments around the world did not care. Today, however all governments recognised the fact that global warming which is threatening life on earth is caused by human activity which is evident from the recently concluded Paris summit on 11th December 2015 on climate change.

The global temperature, at present, stands at 0.69 C. The critical temperature for survival has been pegged at 2 Celsius and might reach before the end of this century, and steps are being initiated to limit the greenhouse gases to below 400ppm. But bringing all nations with varying ideologies on to one platform, to achieve this goal, seems to be a herculean task.

The trouble started with the discovery of fossil fuels which accelerated the industrial revolution as well as greed in man for wealth and comforts. What are most of these industries are doing? They are consuming large quantities of power, water, natural resources as raw materials, and producing products that last for maximum of 10 or 20 years, after that they become waste products. What most industries are doing is, they are converting biodegradable resources into non-biodegradable products which accumulate as waste in the environment and are detrimental to all forms of life. Also, the fossil fuels used by industries as power source, are discharging different greenhouse gases, polluting atmosphere, waters, and causing global warming.

How the industries are making profits? These profits, as it seems, are illusory. Let us consider the example of aircraft industry. Without travelling by air we cannot reach the other side of the globe. This is a luxury and one can reach U.S in less than 20 hours which otherwise takes more than month on ship. But this comfort is so costly and is utilised only by 2 % of the population. But at what cost this luxury is made available.

The aircraft structure is made of special quality high strength aluminium alloy which is obtained by modifying through various stages of metallurgical processes, after the raw material 'bauxite' is extracted from the earth. This mineral is formed in the earth's crust and its source can be traced to star dust out of supernova explosion. The amount of this mineral in the earth's crust is limited which we are extracting and utilising indiscriminately over hundred years. There is pollution during extraction, transportation, refining and utilisation of this mineral.

Economists have not yet devised a formula as how to estimate the cost of this mineral which does not exist forever. We simply add up the extraction and transportation and refining costs and arrive at the final price. The aircraft uses fossil fuel as its power source, all through its flight, it goes on polluting the atmosphere. The jet plume of the aircraft was observed to destroy the delicate ozone layer. The price of the fuel is arrived just like that of bauxite. We do not know how long these fossil fuels are available for us. So if we can take the true cost of materials used to manufacture the aircraft and the true cost of fuel to run, I don't think anyone in this world would afford to fly.

If we analyse every product manufactured and take its true costs no technology is truly economical. Let us put it in another way; no technology is economical and safe for humans and environment. The air we breathe, the water we drink and the food we eat are getting polluted and whom to blame for this. Suppose, each citizen on this planet demands his right to clean air, pure water and clean food, governments, around the world, would start collapsing one after the other.

As discussed earlier, the goal of developing so many technologies is only for improving human comforts. At the same time, no technology is harmless and no technology is economical in the true sense. The economy that is built around the technologies, therefore, is illusory and cannot be sustained for long.

In the near future, scientists and engineers will be engaging themselves in solving the environmental problems that will be threatening our existence. They will be left with no time or resource to pursue any research other than environment which might drastically affect global economy.

2.4 IS SCIENCE AND TECHNOLOGY PANACEA FOR ALL HUMAN PROBLEMS ?

Today, science and technology has become a way of life. It is generating wealth, providing employment, taking care of much needed comforts and improving per capita income. This created an economy of itself, different from agricultural economy. For some people, science is life and panacea for all problems facing humanity. Science and technology is pervading all areas and providing bread and butter to millions and also the required comforts to humanity for transportation, communication, entertainment needs. Medical scientists, though they cannot prevent diseases, providing relief to the diseased.

The question is how long these comforts can be sustained? Is enjoyment of comforts is the only goal, or is there any other goal for human existence?

One should not become a hedonist or solipsist. We must worry about our children and grandchildren, whether they can live on this planet. Instead of preventing damage to our planet, some scientists are planning ways and means to migrate to other planets at least by few people, so that life can continue. This is the height of thinking by scientists; as if they created life, and they feel it is their duty to preserve life.

The problem with current practice of science and technology is, it is branching off into many disciplines, and specialisations, and is ever becoming narrower and narrower. This makes us blind to the totality of the picture. We must encourage multi-disciplinary experts, and encourage only pure sciences.

Our ways of life have seriously affected the ecological balance. We are waking up slowly to the reality of global warming and its consequences. If not arrested, the glaciers start melting raising the sea levels which eventually engulf the coastal areas. It is estimated, recently in 2015, based on studies at NASA, many countries along the coast and island nations might disappear in 100 to 200 years. There might be wars due to shortage of water and food in the next hundred years.

Our technologies and our greed for improving comforts have already affecting the natural bio-chemical cycles that pass through gaseous phase. These include elements like carbon, oxygen, nitrogen, hydrogen, and sulphur. They pass through the atmosphere in transit from one stage to another of their cycle.

Our industrial civilisation, with burning of fossil fuels, has already disturbed these cycles. There is too an increasingly worrying interference with the ozone cycle which is an off-shoot of oxygen cycle. If the ozone in the atmosphere is spread out on the surface of earth it will be mere 3mm thick layer, which is protecting us and plant life from the dangerous ultraviolet radiation from sun. We must understand nature, coexist with nature and not to interfere with its functioning.

Though science and technology are an integral part of our modern culture, they are not a panacea for solving all the problems confronting humanity. If we do not learn to use them with discretion and control they become counterproductive and run contrary to providing basic human needs.

On one side there are rapid developments in engineering and medical science, on the other side our population is multiplying and the quality of our environment is deteriorating, what would be in store for our future scientists and engineers. Most of their time and resources will have to be spent in solving the environmental problems created by indiscriminate practices of present generation scientists and engineers. As if one generation engineers create problems and ask the next generation engineers to solve them. Now we start working on pollution research and control and diagnosing new diseases. Before we could find cure for one disease new one is cropping up.

There are some who argue and express confidence that scientists and engineers can solve all the problems given enough time. This optimism does not stand scrutiny. The solutions must be in tune with nature and not against nature.

Whether it be energy, food, water, air, transportation, communication or health, the researchers must be able to find solutions without any damage to environment or personal health.

Scientists confirmed without any doubt that our planet has entered sixth phase of mass extinction of species. Until the industrial revolution began, the rate of mass extinction stood at 2 species per 10000 per 100 years. Currently, it has jumped to 114 times. That is 228 species per 10000 per 100 years. The reasons mentioned is human activity that is polluting, and causing global warming, and climate change. Every time human activity is being mentioned for generating greenhouse gases that are responsible for global warming. Now it is time to ask who the men behind are? No one dares to mention; because it includes mainly scientists, engineers and industrialists. But mainly scientists and engineers must be held responsible as they cause the environmental damage knowingly, while the commoners are contributing unknowingly.

Science and technology does not serve any purpose when man's personal fate is at stake. Man's personal welfare, his fate and happiness of his kith and kin, depend directly on the outcome of the struggle for peaceful coexistence. In this context, typical questions like: what norms of behaviour must guide man in life? what duties he must perform and what not? What is the purpose of life, and what goal he should set for himself till his death? Can scientists and engineers provide answers or solutions to these questions that arise in human mind? Can our future generations survive and live happily on this planet?

The problem whether the Universe came into existence by accident or is it a design by a Super Natural Power, has bothered scientists ever since science evolved from philosophy. While all religions express their firm belief in God, the Scientists, today, are equally divided on this matter. David C Pack has said that he started believing in God, after studying and comparing various scientific theories. The concepts like matter came into existence from nothing, and life and consciousness evolved from matter are incomprehensible.

3

THE WORLD IS NOT REAL

This world, we see is nothing but the information provided by our eyes, ears, tongue, nose and skin to the mind which creates the picture of the world for us. This book is primarily based on the Advaita Philosophy propounded by Adi Sankaracharya, about two thousand years ago. His entire philosophy can be put into a single sentence as: "Jagat Mithya; Brahma Satyam." This translates into, "The World is an Illusion; God is only Real." Sankaracharya proved his statement based on Upanishads by defining Reality as that which does not undergo any change. Further, anything that comes into existence, and goes out of existence cannot be real. These statements are very difficult to comprehend even by most philosophers and scientists. We are grossly involved, day in and day out, in the worldly affairs, and we refuse to believe that the world in which we are living is not real. However, it is possible to prove the above statement based the present scientific theories such as relativity and quantum mechanical theories.

A closer look at these theories make us doubt whether we are living in a virtual world or a real world. Secondly, we know that space, time and matter, each, can expand or contract, therefore, the world comprising of these three cannot be real, secondly the universe did not exist before the big bang, and goes out of existence one day.

The world in which we are living comprises, basically of four things: space, time, matter. For the time being we ignore living beings or ourselves since we are the observers. The scientists have been exploring, and to our surprise, we come to the feeling that the world we are living is not real, but virtual.

When we are travelling in a train, we observe all the trees, road, etc. appear to be moving backward. If the train is not moving this illusory appearance will disappear. Similarly, if we close our eyes, even though train is moving, the illusory appearance of trees moving backward will disappear. This proves that the illusion is created due to the speed of the train. Secondly, mind is also involved, somehow, in creating this illusion.

Based on such observations, Einstein proposed his relativity theories which established some mind boggling realities which are difficult to comprehend. (Readers who are not familiar with science might skip this chapter)

Also, Einstein had proved that matter can be converted into energy and energy can produce matter; another is that the mass of an object is not same, but increases or decreases with its speed; similarly the length or size of an object depends on its speed. Also 'Time' as we understand does not flow uniformly, but the clock slows down as its speed increases, or when it encounters higher gravitational field. Still more perplexing is the fact that we cannot separate time from space; space-time is one continuum.

The quantum mechanical theories present us further baffling results. Neil Bohr was the first scientist to explore what is inside an atom. The atom comprises of a nucleus at its centre with negatively charged electrons revolving round the nucleus in different orbits possessing different energy levels. The nucleus contained positively charged 'protons,' and neutral particles called 'neutrons'. The number of protons and electrons are equal so that the atom becomes neutral. The atom of every element is different, and contains different number of electrons and neutrons. Thus an atom of iron and an atom of gold is distinguished only by their electron configuration. That is how many electrons are orbiting in which orbit, and how many neutrons are present in the nucleus.

Bohr's model could not explain the black body spectrum for all energy levels. Planck, another physicist, who studied radiation spectrum from black bodies, has observed that the electromagnetic radiation or energy is absorbed or emitted in discrete quantities. He postulated that an atom could absorb or emit energy in lumps or pieces called "Quanta." This energy is proportional to the frequency of the emitted radiation. The proportionality constant is named after him as Planck's constant "h." Einstein discovered that energy $E = m.c^2$, while Planck discovered, $E = h.f.$ Here 'c' is the speed of light, and 'f' is the frequency of electromagnetic radiation.

According to Planck, the energy is quantized; for example, the charge of an electron is 1.6×10^{-19} C, and it is represented as "e." Any charge of a body can be in multiples of 'e' and not as a fraction. Similarly, the energy of an electron is different in different orbits, but it can possess energy in multiples of a smallest energy quanta and not a fraction of it. It is just like how the fare meter of a taxi jumps in quantities of set amount for each kilometre we travel. This quantum approach which explained the puzzle of the black body spectra, laid the road for a new physics called "Quantum Mechanics." According to this approach, two electrons revolving in the same orbit will have different spin directions; that is if one electron revolves in clockwise direction the other must revolve in opposite direction. This way they will have different energy states or quantum states. This was known as Pauli's exclusive Principle.

Heisenberg was another scientist who worked in quantum mechanics and discovered that "It is impossible to know the position and velocity, precisely, of an electron, or any other sub-atomic particle, simultaneously." The act of determining a particle's position was found to disturb its velocity, and the act of finding its velocity is disturbing its position. There were other scientists who tried to evolve quantum mechanical theories: Paul Dirac invented quantum algebra, while Schrodinger invented wave theory to explain quantum mechanical phenomena.

3.1 PARTICLE-WAVE DUALITY

Many scientists struggled to explain the nature of light. It was Newton who tried to explain light propagation by assuming it comprising of particles called corpuscles. He could explain the reflection phenomenon of light, but he failed to explain the phenomenon of interference by two light rays. Later, Huygens was successful in explaining the light interference by assuming light as a wave. These two theories were looked up as two contrasting theories, and created the dilemma whether light is particle or a wave. Compton, in 1920, observed that the interaction between x-rays and electrons could be explained only if x-rays are treated both as a wave as well as a particle in different experiments.

Experiments conducted, based on Einstein's discovery of photo-electric effect, revealed that when a light of specific energy or frequency hits an atom of a certain material, electrons from the atom are thrown out of their orbits and flow into a wire as electric current. Here the momentum of the incident light has resulted in the removal of an electron from its atom. This momentum transfer would not have happened unless light contained particles. Einstein received Nobel Prize for this work. Again interference experiments conducted using two lights waves revealed that the dark and bright fringes on the screen could not result unless light is considered as waves.

3.2 DOUBLE SLIT EXPERIMENT

Young's double-slit experiment in early nineteenth century was very famous. He kept a plate, with two narrow slits, in front of a light source. The two light waves emerging from the two slits interfered with each other, and formed a beautiful bright and dark fringes on a screen kept at a distance. The alternate bright and dark fringes were due to constructive or destructive interference of the two waves. When the crests or troughs of the two interfering waves coincide, it will result in bright spot and is known as constructive interference. On the other hand when the crest of one wave coincides with the trough of the second wave it will result in a dark spot, and is known as destructive interference. This clearly demonstrated that interference can happen only when two waves interact and not when two particle interact. This clearly established the wave nature of light.

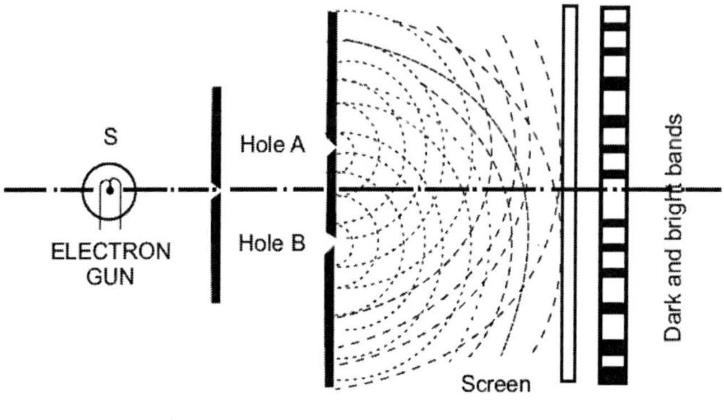

Fig. 3.2 Double Slit Experiment

In another double slit experiment, the light source is replaced by an electron gun as shown in the above figure. To the surprise of all scientists, similar bright and dark fringes were observed on the screen. Everyone knows that an electron is a particle and not a wave. How electron can go through both the slits simultaneously to form interference fringes? When the experiment was conducted with one slit closed, the electron was behaving like an obedient particle going through the slit that is opened. Another experiment was conducted keeping particle detectors at the slits, without blocking their paths. This time again the electrons behaved as particles and no interference was observed. This shows that electrons are behaving like particles when being observed, and behave like waves when not observed. This phenomenon baffled entire scientific community.

Einstein, who quickly grasped the far-reaching consequences of the uncertainty principle and this new phenomenon in physics, vehemently opposed to this particle – wave duality. He seems to have quoted "God does not Play dice" in this context. But Einstein was proved wrong. He was expecting a world whose future can be predicted by knowing the present position and velocity of particles in this universe.

The act of observing is somehow forcing the electron to change its state; particle or wave. The exact path of electron, whether it went through the first slit or the second slit, after it left the source cannot be predicted, but its probability can be predicted mathematically. The quantum theory, as it is usually interpreted, is meaningless without an observer of some sort.

3.3 TWO PHOTON EXPERIMENT

The bizarre nature of photon, a massless particle of light, which remained as a puzzle for a long time has been confirmed by conducting a precise experiment by John Clauser and Stuart Freedman.

Two photons emitted by a single source of light, were made to fly apart in two opposite directions at the speed of light. It is expected that both photons exhibit identical behaviour no matter how far away they were separated. The experiment was conducted by using polarizers. The electric fields of a light wave vibrate in all directions, and perpendicular to the direction of propagation of the wave. A polarizer is a sheet of plastic, which when placed in front of a light source, blocks light waves of all orientations except in one plane. The light coming out of the polarizer is said to be plane polarized. A vertical polarizer, for example, will allow light wave whose electric field is oriented vertically. Similarly, a horizontal polarizer allows light in the horizontal plane and blocks all vertical light waves.

In the two-photon experiment, the polarization of one photon was altered by the experimenter. This action changed the polarization of the second photon instantly.

Repeated experiments proved that the two photons, though separated miles apart from each other, somehow communicating with each other. They remain connected in mysterious way. A particle here, and a particle there, can communicate with each other, instantly, even if they are situated in two different galaxies.

The results of this experiment opened up new possibilities. The experiment conducted elsewhere in the universe can influence the nature of the world, probably life, on this planet. Secondly, if the two photons, separated worlds apart, are instantly communicating with each other, then this communication must travel faster than the speed of light which is prohibited by the barrier imposed by Einstein. These findings put us in a dilemma.

What is the world in which we are living? Scientists like Schrodinger, suggested that the very idea of a unique world, we are living, is itself may be misleading and offered different interpretation. In the double slit experiment using electron, it is suggested, that the possibility of an electron choosing one slit or the other must be considered as happening in two different worlds. In one world the electron goes through the first slit, and in another world the electron goes through the second slit.

The real world is neither of the two worlds, however. The world we experience is the hybrid combination of the above two worlds, each world interfering with each other.

3.4 SCHRODINGER'S THOUGHT EXPERIMENT

The consequences of the double-slit experiments are far-reaching. From afar, the world appear neatly separated into waves and particles, but proves illusory when approached, exhibiting dual nature. Many physicists had received Nobel prizes for their work on quantum mechanics, but the people at large, has not fully digested its implications. Inside the world of atom, there exists perpetual uncertainty in which particles behaviour can be expressed as a set of probabilities, while the reality exists in the eyes of the observer. The laws of physics that hold good in our everyday life are no longer valid in the quantum world. The laws of quantum mechanics defy the laws of Newton and Einstein.

Schrodinger tried to explain the implications of quantum theory by imagining a thought experiment which became very famous and is known as "Schrodinger's cat paradox."

A live cat is kept in a closed box, and in another compartment of the box milk is kept. The two compartments are separated by a door which is designed to open only when a radioactive element decays. Since it is not possible to predict when the radioactive element decays, and since the box is closed, it is not possible to predict whether the cat is alive or dead at any instant. However, according to the probability theory, there are fifty- fifty chance that the cat is alive or dead at any instant of time.

Now we understand the strangeness of the quantum world; neither of the two possibilities open to the cat (dead or alive) has any reality unless the box is opened and observed.

The radioactive decay happened or not, the cat is alive or dead depends only on observation. According to quantum theory, *nothing is real in this world until it is observed.*

The fundamental theoretical quantity in quantum mechanics is the wave function. The wave function is a mathematical entity which allows us to determine the possible outcome of an interaction between an observed system and an observer or an observing system. The wave function is a dynamic description of possible occurrences. The particle-wave duality, according to quantum mechanical theory, is expressed mathematically as a wave function that represents both matter-like as well as wave-like nature of the external world. The world we see is a mixture of both the worlds. Both are equally unreal, and only one of them crystallises as real when observation is made.

We can understand this dual nature in another way; suppose your close friend lives in another country while you live in a different country. Suppose your friend died in an accident, and you get the news only after, say, three months. As far as you are concerned your friend was alive during the last three months. He is dead only when the news reaches you. This news collapsed the wave function of uncertainty (he is alive) and brings you to the reality, he is dead.

3.5 RICHARD FEYNMAN DIAGRAMS

An atom comprises of a nucleus at the centre with electrons revolving around the nucleus. The nucleus comprises of protons and neutrons. Many of us know only these three subatomic particles. In fact, each proton and neutron comprises of three quarks each. These quarks interact with the help of gluons, another type of particles. Electrons interact with each other by exchanging photons, the particles of light. By conducting collision experiments, scientists discovered more than 200 subatomic particles. Subatomic particles are broadly divided into two groups: Hadrons, means heavy particles, and Leptons, means lighter particles. The hadrons are further divided into Baryons (having spin1/2) and Mesons (having spin0). Baryons include Proton, Neutron, Lambda, Sigma, Xi and Omega. The mesons include Pion, Kaon and Eta. The Leptons, the lighter particles are divided into Electrons (having spin1/2) and Neutrinos (having spin0). The Leptons are further divided into Electron, Muon and Tuon, and the Neutrinos are divided into Electron-Neutrino, Muon-Neutron and Tuaon-Neutrino. To explain the radioactive process, through weak interactions, scientists have discovered fermion particles like, W^+, W^-, and Z

These subatomic particles are neither particles nor waves, they are unstable and decay with time. We know the space is three dimensional and time is the fourth dimension. For understanding particle interactions Richard Feynman, who won Nobel Prize for his work in Quantum Electrodynamics (QED), created diagrams, known as Feynman diagrams.

Here three dimensional space is represented along the X-axis while time is represented along the Y-axis. This is known as space-time diagram. In such a diagram a dot represents an *event* in space-time, and a line joining two dots represents a *world line*. A vertical line as shown in the first figure (Fig. 3.2) parallel to Y-axis represents a particle fixed in space and moving in time. Similarly, an inclined line in the space-time diagram represents movement of a particle both in space as well as time.

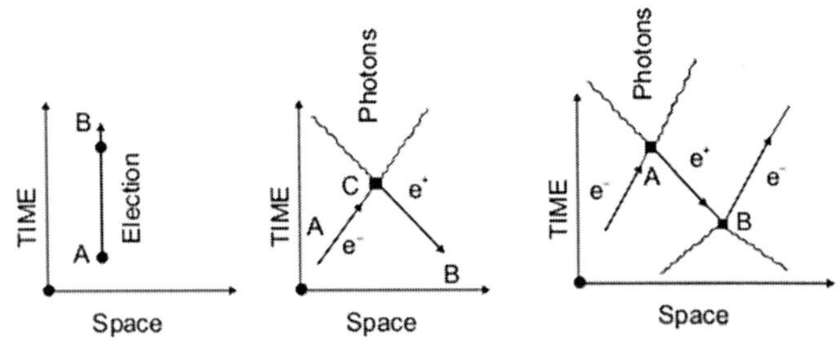

Fig. 3.5 Feynman Diagrams

It was Paul Dirac who discovered anti-matter. When matter and anti-matter come in contact, they annihilate and energy is created instantaneously. Also most of the sub-atomic particles have their anti-particles. For example, positron (e^+) is an anti-particle of electron (e^-). When these two particles meet energy is released. From this energy again particles crop up. The anti-particle of proton is anti-proton.

In the second figure above, a typical electron – positron annihilation is depicted. An electron (e^-) starting from an event A, and a positron (e^+) coming from event B, and both meet at event C and annihilate each other. From the resultant energy two photons are released which move away from each other at the speed of light as shown by the zigzag lines.

In 1949, Richard Feynman discovered that space-time maps like these can have an exact correspondence with mathematical expressions which might be used to estimate the probabilities of particle interactions they depict. However some rules are to be observed in the preparation of the space-time diagrams. A world line carries an arrow mark and represents the movement of a particle or antiparticle. An upward arrow indicates movement of a particle forward in time, while a downward arrow indicates movement of a particle backward in time. The movement of a particle forward in time can be interpreted as backward movement in time of its antiparticle and vice versa. The path of a photon is represented by a zigzag line since it does not need an arrow mark as it has no antiparticle. Secondly, time has no meaning for photon as it travels at the speed of light.

With keeping these rules in mind, let us examine the interaction of subatomic particles as depicted in the third figure above. Two photons collide in the lower right of the diagram at event B. From this energy an electron (e^-) and a positron (e^+) are released which fly away to the right and left respectively. The positron going to the left meets another electron at event

A, and both annihilate each other and in the process create two photons which depart in two different directions.

According to quantum field theory, the events shown in the third figure above can also be interpreted in another way. Here, we consider only one particle. That particle, an electron, enters the diagram from the lower part of the diagram, and travels forward in time and space, and emits two photons at event A. This causes the electron to reverse its direction. So it travels backward in time as a positron, and it absorbs two photons at event B, reverses its direction again and becomes an electron. What we notice in this second interpretation; there is only one particle, where as in the first interpretation there are three particles. Only one particle that moves forward, backward, and again forward in space-time.

Imagine such Feynman diagram that encompasses entire space-time, with track of every particle laid on it. Now imagine viewing this diagram through a narrow slit that allows only limited segment to be scanned, and move the slit steadily up the diagram. Through the slit we see a complex dance of interacting particles; pair productions, annihilations, and far more ever changing panorama. All we are doing is scanning something fixed in space and time. It is our perception, that alters, and not the underlying reality.

Imagine only Pure Consciousness is the Reality, the world we observe is a projection which is constantly undergoing changes due to vibrations of our mind, and so it appears real due to changes in our perception.

There is some evidence to show that consciousness at the most fundamental level is a quantum process. If at the quantum level, the flow of time has no meaning, and if consciousness is fundamentally a quantum process, if we can be aware of these processes within ourselves, then it is conceivable we too can experience timelessness, where ordinary perceptions like space, time and matter may not be applicable. That means a state of enlightenment, transcending space and time, exists in the realm of direct experience.

Happiness is a state of being. That means it exists in the realm of direct experience. The word *happiness* is a word or a symbol to denote the state called happiness. A state of being is an experience. Symbols and experience do not follow the same rules. The discovery that experience and symbols do not follow the same rules has come to the science of physics under the title *quantum logic*. Only one thing exists in this universe that is real and eternal – Pure Consciousness. No two eternal things can coexist. Therefore, everything else in the universe appears to be born or created because of our empirical outlook, but not in reality.

3.6 ARE WE LIVING IN A VIRTUAL WORLD?

Virtual reality is the recent development of a virtual three dimensional environment using advanced computer software, and presenting it to the user who is wearing a special gadget over his head. The user feels as if he is in a totally different world where he can interact with characters or objects projected in the environment, and experiences emotions similar to what he experiences in real life.

The gadget incorporates number of motion sensors in the head, hand and feet, and also eye ball tracking sensors. Out of five senses, three senses like touch, sight and sound have been incorporated. Only one must know what keys have to be pressed on the gadget.

For example, you are flying in an aeroplane in the virtual world. You stretch out both your hands, you take off in the plane. With all the sensory effects, you don't feel any difference between flying in real life and flying in virtual world. You can fly over the ocean or over a city of sky scrapers. When you move your arms together you accelerate your aeroplane, and when you point your arms down you make your plane go down and land. You will experience knee jerk as you land with impact. You may experience nausea or sweating with exhilaration when you move your plane suddenly this way or that way. Virtual reality technology is being developed for virtual marketing, and the real products are delivered to the customer's house by drones. The marketing part is virtual where the customer selects what he wants from the virtual shopping mall, while the delivery is real.

This Virtual Technology is fast advancing, and many companies are bringing out different gadgets into the market. Having proved that the present world itself is not real, is it possible to imagine we are already living in a virtual world!

4

PURPOSE AND GOAL OF LIFE

4.1 PURPOSE OF RELIGION

As earth formed in the solar system, it comprised of 70% oceans and 30% land masses. These land masses have been divided into seven continents, namely, Africa, Antarctica, Asia, Australia, Europe, North America, and South America. Many geographers and scientists now refer to six continents, since Europe and Asia are combined (because they're one solid landmass).

Different civilisations evolved in these continents. There are major ten civilisations: Mesopotamian; Indus Valley; Ancient Egyptian; Mayan; Chinese; Ancient Greek; Persian; Roman; Aztecs and Incas.

A civilization is any complex society characterized by urban development, social stratifications, symbolic communication forms (typically, writing forms), monumental architecture, taxation, societal dependence upon agriculture, and expansionism. Civilizations are organized in densely populated settlements divided into hierarchical social classes with ruling elite and subordinate urban and rural populations, which engage in intensive agriculture, mining, small-scale manufacture and trade. Civilization concentrates power, extending human control over the rest of nature, including over other human beings.

A *tradition* is a belief or behaviour passed down within a group or society with symbolic meaning or special significance with origins in the past. Traditions can persist and evolve for thousands of years

A *culture* is a way of life of a group of people – the behaviours, beliefs, values, and symbols that they accept, generally without thinking about them, and that are passed along by communication and imitation from one generation to the next. Religion is considered as the soul of culture. A religion is an organized collection of beliefs, cultural systems and world views that relate humanity to an order of existence.

There are twelve world religions—those religions most often included in history of world religion surveys and studied in world religions classes: Baha'i, Buddhism, Christianity, Confucianism, Hinduism, Islam, Jainism, Judaism, Shinto, Sikhism, Taoism, and Zoroastrianism.

The question of the origin of religion in the human race still remains one of the insoluble mysteries confronting the mind of man. Many have attempted to solve this problem through scientific research, only to find that the results lead to inevitable antinomies. Like all other questions of "origins," the origin of religion is more a matter of speculation than of investigation; or to make it less extreme, it will at all events be admitted that speculation is involved in a problem for which an entirely satisfactory solution cannot be found through historical investigation.

There is general agreement among cognitive scientists that religion is an outgrowth of brain architecture that evolved early in human history. However, there is disagreement on the exact mechanisms that drove the evolution of the religious mind. We shall still be far from furnishing an answer to the question. How did religion arise? What is it's source?

Many religions have narratives, symbols and sacred histories that aim to explain the meaning of life, the origin of life, or the Universe. From their beliefs about the cosmos and human nature, people may derive morality, ethics, religious laws or a preferred life style. Many religions may have organised behaviours, clergy, a definition of what constitutes adherence or membership, holy, and scriptures. The practice of a religion may include rituals, sermons, commemoration or veneration (of a deity, gods or goddesses), sacrifices, festivals, feasts, trances, initiations, funerary services, matrimonial services, meditation, prayer, music, art, dance, public service, or other aspects of human culture. All world religions are the same, basically conveying the same message that ultimate reality is one God, when we strip their rules, rituals and regulations of their respective faiths.

As societies evolved, morality became important part of religion. Though morality awareness may be a unique human trait, many social animals, such as primates, dolphins and whales, have been known to exhibit pre-moral sentiments. Morality is concerned with attachment and bonding, cooperation and mutual aid, sympathy and empathy, direct and indirect reciprocity, altruism and reciprocal altruism, conflict resolution and peace-making, deception and deception detection, community concern and caring about what others think about oneself, and awareness of and response to the social rules of the group. Social order is maintained by certain rules of expected behaviour and dominant group members enforce order through punishment and fear of God.

The latest research has shown that animal communities also observe morality. If a one member is dead all join to express their feelings, a recent study has found that birds sacrifice food for the sake of love.

The purpose of religion, especially the oldest Hindu religion seems to be four fold: The first one is to inculcate discipline in the society. Today we see law and order is maintained by the police and legal system. These come into action only after an illegal act or crime has taken place. But religion aims to transform the human mind before he becomes antisocial or commits a sin or crime. If governments want to prevent crimes or antisocial behaviour, they need to post one policeman against one citizen. This becomes an impossible task. The Holy books of all religions contain rules and regulations, do's and don'ts, the concepts of sin and virtue, hell and heaven and fear of God. Thus a religion can bring in discipline among its citizens. The religious merit is known as *dharma.* The concept of dharma is central to the Hindu philosophy and religion. *Dharma* means 'right way of living' and 'path of righteousness' that was established. Anything that harms an individual, society or environment is considered against dharma.

Dharma in Hinduism, is an organizing principle that applies to human beings in solitude, in their interaction with human beings and nature, as well as between inanimate objects, to all of cosmos and its parts. For example, "Save the Trees, trees will save you" is one established dharma. Now, we know how relevant is this in the present day we are coming to know how deforestation is causing global warming with irreversible consequences. It refers to the order and customs which make life and universe possible, and includes behaviours, rituals, rules that govern society, and ethics. Hindu dharma includes the religious duties, moral rights and duties of each individual, as well as behaviours that enable social order, right conduct, and those that are virtuous.

There is something unique about Indian culture which can be identified with a single word: Integration. *Sanatana Dharma* is the main centre of Indian culture. Here, life, religion, society, physical world, people of different V*arnas, and Ashrams,* the past, present and even future are seen as an integrated whole. The Indian education system was the oldest, and it teaches the role of a man in the society as well as his goal towards the end of his life.

According to Indian Vedanta, everything we see around, including human beings comprise of only five elements: *Akas* or space, *Vayu* or air, *Fire* or radiation, *jalam* or water, and *dharti* or earth. Everything in the universe is the creation of Spirit. The human body also comprises of these five elements. So, Indians worship, all the five elements involved in the creation, as gods or goddesses. For example, the wind sweeps everything. The fire burns up everything that comes into its contact. There is also the vital breath which activates living beings. But all these are moved by a Spirit. This Spirit is not created by any one. It exists by itself. And yet it creates and sustains the creation. Thus the entire creation is a complex instrument that is carried out at the behest of the Spirit.

The second purpose of a religion is to guide its citizens how to earn and live in the society keeping sin and virtue in mind. Every citizen must involve in a social activity in order to earn his livelihood. If we look at carefully and analyse, there are only four modes of earning for one's livelihood. This is based on what the society needs for its survival. They are known as *protector*, *preacher* or teacher, *feeder*, and *social worker*. People choose one of the four professions to earn their livelihood. In fact, any society, even today, survives by the services of these four categories of people, and we cannot find a fifth profession. These professions, over a period, have become family professions as they acquired skills. These professions, for some, also became their identity and family names. According to Hinduism, these four 'vernas' are the four pillars of the society. Later on, these four Vernas became 4000 castes, which are nothing but the creation by people of different Vernas dividing among themselves, based on habits and faiths.

Thus the society was divided into four *Vernas*, depending on the profession one choses to earn his livelihood. First, the society needs a leader or a king who is physically strong, and who can influence a group of people to follow him and involve in activities to protect the society from external threats and ensure peace in the society. This leader and his followers are taken care by the society for their survival. Such a person is known as *Kshatriya*.

Secondly, the society needs a priest to look after the rituals at the places of worship, and to conduct ceremonies during functions like birth of a child, marriages or death of a person. He is supposed to be most knowledgeable man in the society, conversant with Holy books, and capable of clarifying any doubts that arise in the inquisitive mind of the citizens by preaching and teaching. He too is paid by the society for his services. Such a class of people is known as *Brahmin* or Priest.

The citizens of the society requires food grains, milk, vegetables, fruits etc. for their day to day needs. The person who caters to such needs of the society is known as *Vysya*. His job is to gather and provide the daily needs of the society. He earns his livelihood by providing the necessities of the people of the society.

The fourth class of the society looks after the needs of all members of the society by providing services such as farming, house construction, etc. He is service oriented and capable of helping others by his physical strength. This class is known as *shudra*.

For this reason, these four classes of society were known as the four pillars of the society. It is possible one person from one class can adapt to another class, but these four classes exist at all times. Persons of these classes can earn by following the rules and regulations of the society. Cheating, stealing, lying, dishonesty are all considered acts of sin and are prohibited. All the four classes of people are equal in the eyes of the God, and are eligible for religious rituals and spiritual progress. This goal of earning for living and material possessions, following their professions and adhering to dharma, is known as *Artha.*

In a similar manner, the duties of a man in different stages of his life such as childhood, bachelor life, married life, and retired life have been specified. These are known as *ashram dharmas* and mainly consist of dos and don'ts. The individual during retired life must fully dedicate to the spiritual path of knowledge after the age of sixty.

The third purpose of religion is with regards to how to fulfil one's desires without greed. Our five senses only create the world for us. In this world we try to find happiness. This happiness has two main sources. One is, we form relationships with our kith and kin, and in the process we try to find happiness. The second source is the objects in this materialistic world. We get happiness by possessing them. However, it must be remembered that we have to pay a price to get theses joys. If we get happiness from marriage and children, we have to pay price, and similarly, if we want to possess any goods of our interest we have to pay price. Even after paying a price for our possessions, the happiness does not last long. New desires keep on propping up. If we analyse closely, we come to the conclusion that the happiness and joys we derive from relationships and material possessions cannot provide lasting peace. One must learn how to be in peace with oneself.

Therefore, one's happiness depends on contentment. The nature of desire is such, when one desire is fulfilled another desire is ready in the mind. People must have clear understanding of how the desires arise one after another. After the basic needs through his lively hoods are met, the man desires for a wife and family starts; then the desire for a house, car, etc. There is nothing wrong in these desires. One should not be disturbed mentally if one desire is not fulfilled. Otherwise this will lead to anger and frustration. He should not involve in illegal or immoral acts to earn more to fulfil his unreasonable desires. When there is no contentment the desire leads to greed.

The desires mostly sought after by majority of people are to strive for wealth, fame, power, and recognition. When a man has greed, then he is likely to deviate from virtuous path to meet the above goals. One must understand that wealth, fame and power, one gets or not depend very much on his karmas performed in his previous births. One must know if a man is wealthy, it is because of his karma(actions) in his previous births; if one has earned Nobel prize, remember it as due to karma of previous births; if one is born poor or handicapped, remember as the result of previous karma. Therefore one should not be greedy for them. If they come accept, if not take it easy having known the reasons.

Suppose a man wanted to buy a luxury car which he longed to buy, but could not afford; when he finds his very neighbour purchased the very same car he will be engulfed in jealousy and frustration. The main problem with most of us is the fact that we tune our lives in comparison with our neighbours or colleagues. Anger, greed and jealousy can drive a man to such an extent he might resort to stealing, cheating and other criminal acts. This will lead to his down fall. Therefore, honesty and contentment are the qualities one should strive for in order to reach his goal. This third goal, which meets the gratifications of his senses, is known as *Kama.*

The fourth and last purpose of religion is to guide man to his liberation or *Moksha.* This requires physical and mental discipline. In other words purity of the mind, absence of desires and ego, and clarity in the intellect is essential. Only knowledge can give him lasting peace of mind or bliss, and ensure liberation (moksha) to unite him with God after death so that he is not reborn again and again. This is because the highest knowledge alone is eternal like God. Rituals, worships and prayers at temples, churches and mosques are required, and they help in purifying the mind and body. Since these are classified as actions, the result may also be in the form of materialistic benefits, but not moksha. Therefore, rituals and prayers not only purifies one's mind but also induce the young children to lead a discipline life later in their adulthood.

When the mind becomes pure, and intellect sharp, he becomes eligible to gain Ultimate knowledge or Self-knowledge. One should consider the rituals and prayers and worship as stepping stones to the final goal, the Blissful state and liberation. This Self-knowledge is nothing but a close analysis of how the desires, feelings of happiness or frustration generate in the mind. The root cause for the all the ills facing man is man himself and his ignorance, which can be removed only by right knowledge.

A philosophical attitude to life is essential to control one's ego. After learning how small he is on this planet compared to the size of the universe, how inevitable is the death which is constantly chasing him. This knowledge makes one shed his ego, and gives him confidence and ability to understand the illusory nature of the world. Understanding how fragile our relationships with our kith and kin and how they are all mere mental precepts, provides one the necessary detached attitude towards the materialistic world.

Today, as it looks, many people are trying to live longer by all means. He goes to gym, spends lot of money for health. One should not be misled or misguided forgetting life's goal. Physical health and mental health are needed to obtain the knowledge. Knowledge must be the main goal, and not living many years into old age.

The knowledge of a person guides one's thoughts. The thoughts of a person shapes his attitude. The attitude of a person decides his behaviour. The behaviour of a person decides his destiny.

Just like a rocket or a missile is guided to its target by making it follow the prescribed path, and any deviations occurring due to wind or other cause are immediately corrected by activating control systems. In a similar way, the goal must be kept in view always, and any deviations must be corrected immediately. Once he understands ultimate knowledge, he transcends death, he fears death or diseases no more since he gets enlightened with knowledge about the root causes. This fourth goal is known as *Moksha.*

4.2 HAPPINESS

If you take a survey across the educated and employed in the urban cities around the globe, and ask the question "what for you are living" you get no answer. This is because most of us live a life without a defined goal or purpose. It looks strange, as we do introspection about why people lead a life without any ultimate purpose or goal. If we look into the animal kingdom, or every living being on this planet, one observes their constant effort and strive to maximise their happiness. It seems, animals on this planet are living more happily than human beings. They hunt for food only when they are hungry, and play and sleep, rest of the time. Their desires are limited, and they find their comfort in the natural environment. But it is only man who eats even when he is not hungry and can fast even when he is hungry. His desires grow day by day and is ready to go to any extent to improve his comfortable living, and imagines they provide him the needed happiness. So, what is happiness?

Economists, around the world use Gross Domestic Product and per capita income to assess which country is progressing at what rate. Off late, this view is gradually changing. Every human being, including animals, living on this planet has a natural instinct to maximise their happiness. Recognising this fact, United Nations General Assembly, in 2012, declared April 24th as the International day of Happiness. All of us know the same body declared June 21st as the International Yoga day based on the proposal made by India's Prime Minister Narendra Modi last year.

On the International Happiness Day, every year, a research team conducts survey and rank the nations. They consider factors like health, life expectancy, freedom of choices in addition to GDP and per capita income of citizens to determine people of which country are the happiest. Their assessment presented on April 24th 2015, puts the country Switzerland as number one followed by Iceland, Denmark, Norway and Canada. Most unhappy people lived in countries like Togo, Burundi, Benin and Rwanda.

India is put at number 117. What is surprising is the fact that India is behind countries like Pakistan (81), Palestine (108) and Bangladesh (109). This is despite the fact India was considered as a Spiritual nation, and Yoga centre of the world. This requires serious thinking by our politicians, and introspection by one and all. But still we need to know what happiness is and how to improve.

We all learn, in the childhood, the rhyme "Early to bed and early to rise, makes man healthy, wealthy and wise." If you analyse this carefully we get some clue. To be happy one needs to have good health, wealth and also wisdom. Suppose one is wealthy but has poor health, he cannot be happy. Similarly, if one has good health but very poor, he cannot be happy. Even though one has good health as well good wealth, if he does not have wisdom he cannot be happy. By selecting and eating junk foods, he may lose his health, and by investing unwisely he may lose his wealth.

Therefore, to be happy, one must have health, wealth and wisdom in equal proportion and above average. Further, if there is no contentment, even the wealthiest man in the world cannot be happy. That is why it is said: "Happiness is inversely proportional to the square of his desires."

Lastly, if a person's mentality is such that he keeps on brooding over the mistakes committed in the past or worrying about the future that is unknown, he can never be happy. That is why happiness is defined as: "The state of mind where the past and future are absent." If every citizen is aware of what is happiness, then happiness index of the people around the globe can be improved in the years to come.

The happiness we have been talking about is relative. One may feel happy at this moment, and suddenly go into depression in the next moment when he hears a bad news about loss of his health or wealth. Is it possible for a man to be happy under all circumstances? Philosophers pondered over this for centuries. The happiness has been quantized and recorded in the ancient Hindu scriptures.

If the happiness of a healthy, wealthy, and strong man on this planet is taken as one unit, the happiness of the departed souls staying in different worlds are mentioned thus:

The happiness of Ajana Deva is 100 times the happiest human being; the happiness of Karma Devas is 100 times compared to Ajana Devas; the happiness of Devas is 100 times that of Karma Devas; The happiness of Indra Deva is 100 times that of Devas; the happiness of Brihaspati is 100 times that of Indra; the happiness of Lord Brahma is 100 times that of Brihaspati; finally the happiness of the enlightened person through Self-knowledge is 100 times that of Brihaspati.

Thus the man who understood his true nature as Pure Consciousness, his happiness is more than trillion times, and that is why it is called Bliss. This is the main attraction to pursue Self-knowledge, and it is not a figment of imagination, but many great souls achieved and the records are available,

It is possible for one to make an attempt to understand the ground reasons for his happiness or sorrow. For this one has to understand about the working of his own mind. Here we need a distinction between our physical brain and mind as discussed already. For Bliss one has to learn the Truth in a systematic way.

4.3 PHILOSOPHY IS MORE THAN SCIENCE

Albert Einstein, after understanding the limitations posed by the quantum uncertainty principle hypothesised by Heisenberg in 1938, wrote about the scope of understanding of our universe thus:

"Physical concepts are free creations of the human mind, and not, however it may seem, uniquely determined by the external world. In our endeavour to understand reality we are somewhat like a man trying to understand the mechanism of a closed watch. He sees the face and moving hands, even hears its ticking, but has no way of opening the case. If he is ingenious, he may form some picture of the mechanism which could be responsible for his observations, but he never be quiet sure his picture is the only one which could explain the observations. He will never be able to compare his picture with the real mechanism and he cannot even imagine the possibility of such a comparison."

Even though, many theories proposed after this statement, but the unknown remains the same. In fact, in the pursuit of empirical science, more and more unknowns have come to light such as dark matter and dark energy while scientists are hypothesising theories after theories to understand the origin of our universe. The particle-wave duality, mind-body mystery are yet to be resolved. There seems to be limitations to the progress of science. There is no single scientific theory or law without certain basic assumptions. This shows science is only abstract, and it cannot comprehend Reality which is absolute.

Philosophy, as a form of theoretical knowledge seeks to provide tenets of man's relationship with the environment and present them in a consistent manner. The foundations of any philosophical doctrine is aimed at generalisation, based on a systematic analysis of a vast number of facts pertaining to the most diverse spheres of man's life and activities in a scientific manner. For this reason, philosophy can be regarded as "science."

From the beginning of nineteenth century, man's knowledge of the physical world gradually expanded, and science branched off into many areas like, physics, chemistry, mathematics, biology, astronomy, etc. However, this knowledge of science, are not able to provide any solutions to many of the problems faced by ordinary people. What is happiness, why man has to experience sorrow and misery, why he is helpless? What is life and death? What is the purpose of life? What are his duties? Why he must obey his conscience? Any amount of scientific knowledge cannot answer these questions, and it does not serve any purpose when man's personal fate is at stake.

Science and technology provides only comforts and nothing more. These are being provided at the high cost of environmental damage which is threatening our existence. Is this what a man in the society wants? As discussed earlier, man must be able to live happily. In fact this is the goal of all species on this planet. To provide happiness to man, all his doubts in his mind must be resolved first. Only philosophy has answers to the problems faced by man. For this additional reason philosophy can be called as "science of science."

The process of cognition, according to theory of knowledge or epistemology, starts with the impressions or images received through our five sense organs. The eyes, ears, nose, skin and mouth are the five sense organs of man which enable him to come in contact with the external world. The information from the senses reaches the brain, and after processing, the mind projects the knowledge about the objects distinguishing colours (red or green), form and size (tree or a mountain), sounds (music or whisper), sensations (smooth or rough) and taste (bitter or sweet). However, there are limits to the senses in gathering information. We cannot see objects in infrared or ultraviolet colours; we cannot see molecules or atoms; we cannot hear sound outside the audible range; we cannot sense earth's magnetic field.

The number of sense organs, their intensity and range depended on the nature and manner of existence of living organisms. The sense organs, according to the theory of evolution, perceive that which is vitally important for the living being in order to orient itself in this world. For example a bee can perceive the form that resembles a flower, but it cannot distinguish geometrical shapes like circle or triangle. Man is the only animal blessed with ability to reason based on sensual information. He is also able to express his attitude towards the external world. Our sensual impressions are connected with thinking. Ancient philosophers, and modern scientists, though unable to see atoms, could imagine that the world is made up of atoms.

A concept or idea is a more complex form of sensual cognition. It is impression of an object which is not perceived immediately. For example, we have the images of people or places acquainted or visited in our mind. These concepts or ideas emerge due to the functioning of the memory. Sometimes one and the same object may be perceived by different people differently. Suppose three people visit Paris and see places together, then when they come back, they describe their experiences differently. One may describe the city traffic, another about the architecture and yet another about the culture of the French people. The ideas and concepts are influenced by man's previous knowledge, experience, types of activity, and his needs and feelings. These concepts and ideas do not themselves contain all the properties of the objects, but man extracts knowledge from the features which provide a deeper and more general picture of the world. Thinking helps create imaginary concepts and ideas. For example, we see an artist's imagination in his painting, or read a science fiction in a novel. However, do the sensual impressions provide us with the correct knowledge?

This epistemological question created interest in philosophers in ancient times. Some thought the world we perceive is as real as it appears. But most others felt differently. For example, the size of the object changes depending on the angle and distance from which we perceive it. Illusions are also caused due to the conditions and environment under which we are looking at it. For example, the appearance of mirage, the bending of a spoon, when immersed in water. Based on observations of such illusions, many philosophers felt that knowledge must be based not on information provided by our senses but by reasoning. Sensations, therefore, give us the information about the external world while the mind, with its ability to think and reason, serves to cognise the internal properties and their inter-relationships or connections. For example, we can see glow of an electric lamp, but we cannot see the current as flow of electrons in the wire. We can see a falling apple but not the force of gravity that cause it.

To understand these hidden phenomena we need a thinking mind. When we see a stranger, we can observe only his external features like short or tall, fair or dark. These external features do not give us detailed information such as race, age, nativity and habits. The detailed information can be obtained only by thinking, comparison, abstraction and reasoning. Ideas reflect the changing world and therefore themselves undergo changes.

New concepts like rockets and space travel arise as thinking advances. Physics, for example, revealed new properties of matter that were not apparent earlier.

Speech and language are also forms of thinking. By speech we not only denote an object but its salient features. When one speaks of an orange, it immediately causes not only its size and colour but also its taste. Language, similarly, does not only denote but expresses thoughts. For example, a novel is not simply an assemblage of letters and words; it induces thoughts and emotions in the reader.

Judgements and deductions are advanced form of thinking. A judgement is linkage of two or more concepts when one is characterised through the other. For example, primitive man learnt to produce fire by friction. But ages passed before the scientific judgement was made that friction is a source of heat. Right Brothers were successful in building a flying machine, but decades passed before aerodynamic theory is advanced. Further advanced thinking led to the development of passenger and fighter jets.

A chain of judgements may lead to a new form of thinking known as deduction. New knowledge is deduced from the accumulated knowledge or experience. Newton's laws of motion or Einstein's theories of relativity are some examples of deductions arrived at careful generalisation by the process of thinking and reasoning. Similarly, we come across many mathematical deductions.

Under the subject of epistemology, the theory of knowledge has been dealt with by many great philosophers. Most eminent among them in the east were Adi Sankaracharya, and Ramanujacharya. Among the western scholars, Plato and Immanuel Kant made significant contributions. Cognitive science, which is being advanced during the last few decades, is the result of integration of multidisciplinary sciences that deal with different sense organs of perception. They try to answer questions like; what it means to know, and to have accurate beliefs, or to be ignorant or to be mistaken. They are researching into the source of knowledge, and consciousness. They are curious about differences among individuals: what can be known by a child, an adult or an individual who has suffered a brain damage or a mature scientist? Further, a cognitive scientist is interested in various vehicles of knowledge; what is a form, an image, a concept, a word? And how these modes of representation relate to one another. The invention of computer came handy to the cognitive scientists. They were able to develop robots and humanoids that are able to perform various tasks. They often consider and compare human body to that of a machine. Even if scientists could design a machine as complex as human body that machine will not be able to resemble the complex human mind with its creative power.

Two fundamental problems are confronting the modern cognitive scientists: How do optical illusions persist even after they have been recognised as illusory? The second one relates to the simulation of human behaviour on a computer. Man is a social animal. His behaviour not only depends on his genes and brain function, but also depends on socioeconomic conditions, political, environment, and religious connections, friends, parents, teachers and finally the knowledge he acquired. The human mind is a unified thing and is not decomposable.

The process of cognition, its levels and forms, is characterised by man's ability to penetrate deeper into the secrets of the universe and brain to achieve new knowledge. This is the essence of creative activity of man. But what is creativity? It is associated with creation of something new. But can man is capable of creating anything new? With advancement of science and technology man has learnt to transform the resources available on the planet into so many products of his necessity and interest. But can he create matter, planets or another universe?

The study of creative act is complex, because new knowledge often appears suddenly, by way of 'revelation', a sudden penetration of the essence. This has led to the contraposition of the two sides of creativity; the 'conscious' which is determined by thinking and the 'subconscious' not directly governed by thinking but by deeper hidden process - "intuition."

4.4 LIFE AFTER DEATH

If there is no life after death, most of the religions which express faith in heaven and hell and reincarnation, will collapse like a pack of cards. If there is no life after death, one need not be bound by the feelings of sin and virtue; honesty and honour. In fact, if corruption and stealing are legalised, we can achieve socialism overnight. But this is not the case. Most people express faith in constitution of their country. Constitutions of all most all countries were written based on the religious principles, and religions, invariably believe in life after death. So the big question is how to comprehend this belief?

If we assume Darwin's theory of evolution is right, we must observe the evolution of all species to the same degree. For example, when we compare two human beings, they are equally evolved in terms of organisational complexity. However in the real world we observe one is mean and selfish, while the other is magnanimous and altruistic. One is wicked while the other virtuous. These observations force us to believe that one is more evolved than the other.

According to Gary Zukav, who authored the book " The seat of the soul," the evolution of a human being with five senses, the physical environment around us is seen in terms of physical survival as the fundamental criterion. Therefore, the goal of life seems to acquire power, by all means, to control the environment and the people within it. The perception of this external power is the main driving force behind our economies, and money has become the symbol of this external power. Struggle for this power is responsible for dividing the nations, creating wars and violence, and ultimately bring only pain and destruction.

Apart from the external power, there is one 'Authentic Power" or internal power within in each one of us. This power is behind the love we express, the compassion we show to fellow human beings, the power that loves life in every form, and provides a meaning and purpose to our lives. Unlike the external power, this internal power cannot be bought, inherited or hoarded. This power comes from the soul whose attributes are love, compassion and wisdom. This soul is not a passive or a theoretical entity that can be traced to the cavity of the heart, it is a positive and purposeful force that guides our destiny. This soul has full energy before it starts taking births.

All the ill thoughts, actions and pain we experience are nothing but loss of energy of the soul, and finally the soul returns back to the source when it regains its full energy after experiencing many births.

According to ecological principles, death is recycled in nature; without death there is no life. In an ecological system, the species constantly exchange, matter, energy and information struggling for space under the sun and competing with each other for food. Biotic circulation involving synthesis and destruction of organic matter is essential for the organisation of life. The organic matter produced due to photosynthesis is to be balanced by its consumption by the organisms and animals. All living beings never exhibit equilibrium and are constantly working at the expense of their free energy to prevent equilibrium as required by the laws of physics and chemistry. Indeed at the level of organisms, life is known to proceed by a constant replacement of individuals; some organisms perish while others are born. That is, synthesis and destruction of molecules, birth and death of individuals or appearance and extinction of species. In other words life comes into existence only where there is death of species.

There is some experimental proof to show that in a complex ecosystem, there is no overall population explosion. The death rate of older species and the birth rate new ones are more or less same. Each one of us can also do some introspection with our common sense. We, human beings are coexisting with all other forms of species, all animal kingdom, flora and fauna. For example, we see dogs and cats and other animals in our daily life. Think for a moment what made them to be born as animals and what made us to be born as human beings. We also see the level difference in evolution. What conclusion can we draw from these observations?

We observe child prodigies showing unbelievable performances in all fields of arts such as music, painting and science. In psychology research literature, the term 'child prodigy' is defined as person under the age of ten who produces meaningful output in some domain to the level of an adult expert performer. We simply say they are blessed. Is there more to it? The story of Tanishq Abraham is a case in point. An Indian-American home-schooled boy has surprised one and all by graduating from a US college at the age of 11 with three associate degrees in maths, science and foreign language studies. Tanishq Abraham, a native of Sacramento, California, graduated from American River College in Sacramento (ARC), California, alongside 1,800 students. Abraham is the youngest person to graduate from American River College this year. President, Barack Obama had sent Tanishq a congratulatory letter. His IQ was high even when he was four-year old. Unless knowledge passed on to the child from his previous birth it is difficult to explain such instances. Yet another case, Tristan

Pang (born 2001), started reading independently and doing high school math at the age of two, and appeared for the Cambridge International examinations IGCSE math when he was 11 years and earned the top grade of A*, At the age of 13 he started his university studies at the University of Auckland and created a free online learning platform.

We come across a lot of make-believe stories of children narrating about their previous life. In fact, now a day's, lot of research is going on about reincarnation based on such stories. The story of James Leininger is truly stunning. Since birth, James was obsessed with airplanes and as a young child started having dreams about flying, weapons, and plane accidents. One day, shortly after the nightmares started, James started to recall his previous life as a fighter pilot. Eventually, James was able to share more details about his past life with his parents, such as: the name of the pilot, James M. Huston Jr.; the Navy ship on which he served, the Natoma; his co-pilot's name; and the fact that he was shot down at Iwo Jima. With just a little effort, James' father was able to track down Huston's co-pilot Jack Larson and Huston's living sister. From that point forth, the boy was able to recall events and people from Huston's life with such clarity, that there was no reason for his family and Huston's sister not to believe him.

Dr. Brian Weiss, is a psychiatrist who lives and practices in Miami, Florida. He is author of the bestselling book "Same Soul, Many Bodies" and narrates the stories of his patients whom he treated using the technique known as 'past life regression'. He finds solution to his patient's current problem by relating it to events in one of his past lives.

Under hypnosis, he observed patients, when regressed to one of their previous births, they start speaking the foreign language of that country where they were born. Since they do not have an iota of knowledge of that language in the present life, he calls such a phenomenon as *Xenoglossia* and says as an excellent proof that the patients are telling true stories of their previous lives.

The study and research on Near Death Experiences of about 150 case studies was presented by Raymond Moody in his book "Life after Life" which was published in 1975. Near Death Experience Research Foundation (NDERF) is dedicated to the study and sharing of case studies. Recently, Scientists at the University of Southampton spent four years examining more than 2000 people who suffered cardiac arrest near around 15 hospitals in the UK, US and Austria. Nearly 40 percent of people who survived described some kind of 'awareness' during the time when they were declared clinically dead before their hearts were restarted. One man even recalled leaving his body entirely and watching his resuscitation from the corner of the room, researchers said. In yet another case, a 57 year old social worker from Southampton, who was dead for three minutes, recounted the actions of the nursing staff in detail.

Dr. Sam Parnia feels that brain cannot function when the heart has stopped beating. But in this case conscious awareness appears to have continued for three minutes into the period when the heart was not beating, even though the brain typically shuts down within 20–30 seconds after the heart has stopped. He said the details he provided during this period was incredible and factual.

Out of the 2060 cases of cardiac arrest patients studied, 330 survived while 140 said they had experienced some kind of awareness while being resuscitated. One in five said they had felt an unusual sense of peacefulness while nearly one-third said time had slowed down or speeded up. Some recalled seeing a bright light; a golden flash or the sun shining. Others recounted feeling of fear or drowning or being dragged through deep water. These studies published in the journal of "Resuscitation" conclusively established the fact that consciousness of a person can exist outside his body even after death.

According to the Indian Scriptures, when a person dies, the physical body perishes, but the subtle body comprising of the mind, intellect ego and memory, departs the body and takes birth again, incarnating another physical body. The subtle body carries with it all 'Samskaras' that include information about his good deeds, bad deeds and knowledge he gained, which become the seed for the next life. Just like we copy all the files from a computer hard disc into a pen drive and carry it to another place. The subtle body that leaves the gross body, at the time of death, is sometimes referred as Jiva. The sequence of death as described is as follows: first senses stop functioning, followed by brain and mind, then breathe stops heart. Then the (Jiva) subtle body leaves the dead physical body along with breathe or prana.

The rebirth of an individual is due to the following four types of seeds: *Samvedana* means inclination of a person towards sense objects; *Bhavanam,* means a person keeps on thinking even when the objects are not in sight; *Vasana,* which means *fixation* of the mind on the materialistic objects and determination to possess them at any cost; *Kalana*, means craving for one's body, kith and kin even while on the death bed. Last minute desire to live more is the main seed of rebirth. If a person could understand that his true nature is Pure Consciousness, and the world is an illusion, he will not take birth again.

The story of a Rishi by name Jada Baharat is mentioned in the scriptures in order to highlight this point. In order to gain liberation from repeated births and deaths, he retires to a forest to do penance. One day, a deer with an arrow pierced into its body enters his hermit, supposedly targeted by an unknown hunter. The Rishi, out of pity, nourishes the deer and takes care of it until deer fully recovered. The deer refuses to leave him, and the Rishi is fascinated by its love and nourishes it with more and more affection. The Rishi, forgot his purpose of coming to forest, and when he died he was born as a deer in his next life.

Ancient Indian Rishis who researched on themselves by observing how the mind passes through the three conscious states, namely waking, dream and deep-sleep. In deep-sleep the mind does not function. We may feel there are breaks in our consciousness. However, the consciousness is a continuous stream. Consider, for example, you were reading a book yesterday during waking state and you completed, say, reading 29 pages. Then you went to sleep, passing through dream and deep sleep states. Today you woke up and start reading the book from page 30. This is not possible unless there is continuity in the consciousness. This means consciousness exists outside the mind, and the assumption by the scientists that consciousness evolved from matter does not stand the scrutiny.

One Russian Scientist, who has been researching on bio-energy fields surrounding living beings, had claimed he had photographed the soul leaving the body at the time of death of a man. His techniques of photography involves what are known as Kirlian photography, and Gas Discharge Visualisation. Dr. Konstantin Korsakov photographed a person at the moment of his death, with a bio-electrographic camera as well as with gas discharge visualisation method, photographed the life force of the person leaving the body gradually.

According to Korotkov, navel and head are the first to lose their life force (soul), while groin and the heart are the last areas.

This technique developed by Korotkov, who is the director of Research Institute of Physical Culture, St. Petersburg, is endorsed as a medical technology by the Ministry of Health of Russia, and is used by more than 300 doctors in the world for monitoring the progress of patients treated for diseases such as cancer. He claims, this technique could be used to watch all kinds of energy imbalances in the patients and diagnose in real time by amplifying the energy fields (Aura) using electromagnetic field. There is ample proof to prove that life exists after death, and the goal of human life is how to present future births.

5

SANKARA THE GENIUS

5.1 BIRTH OF A GREAT PHILOSPHER

Adi Sankaracharya, familiarly known as Sankara, was the founder of the great Advaita Philosophy. He is the one of the keenest minds in the firmament of medieval Hindu philosophy, and a mighty force in the restitution of many thoughts and beliefs, many scriptural writings and metaphysical subtleties that date back to pre-Christian era.

Sankaracharya was born in a small village called Kaladi, situated in the Kerala state of southern India. There are conflicting reports about his date of birth. According to one source, he was born on 25th March, 44 B.C. According to another version, he lived between 820 – 780 AD. It was well known fact that Sankara was very much upset about the wide spread popularity of Buddhism which was threatening the existence of Hindu religion during the regime of Emperor Asoka. It was believed that he succeeded in demolishing the Buddhism by his arguments, he engaged prominent Buddhist Scholars and defeated them. From these facts, his birth date of 25th March 44 B.C seems to be more reliable. More than his existence, his revolutionary philosophical concepts which he was able to successfully and logically present is important. Today, even scientists might find it difficult to counter his doctrine.

Sankara, not only synthesized all the philosophies and ideals, but he purified them. Sometimes, when a creed of religions goes down the centuries, it gathers immaterial rituals and accreditations which were mistaken for the essence of a religion. He broke that crust and went to the essence of all those religions existing in his period, and showed how they all could be synthesized and they fall into one pattern.

Sankara's father died when he was very young. His mother performed his *Upanayana,* the ceremony to make him eligible for studying Vedas. He studied Vedas, Upanishads and Brahmasutra under his guru, Govindapada, and authored several key works in his youth, while he was still a student. It is with his teacher that Sankara studied 'Gaudapadiya Karika;' it is most important to mention was the fact that he happened to meet, on different occasions, great scholars of the *Mimamsa* school of thought of Hinduism namely, Kumarila and Prabhakara, as well as Mandana Misra as well as various Buddhist scholars. He participated in a number of *Shastrarth* (an Indian tradition of public philosophical debates attended by large number of people, sometimes with royalty).

While the details and chronology of events vary, most biographies mention Adi Sankara traveling widely within India, Gujarat to Bengal, and participating in public philosophical debates with different orthodox schools of Hindu philosophy, as well as heterodox traditions such as Buddhists, Jains, Arhatas, Saugatas, and Carvakas. Adi Sankara had a number of scholars who became his disciples during his travels. These include Padmapada (also called Sanandana, associated with the text *Atma-bodha*), Sureshvara, Tothaka, Citsukha, Prthividhara, Cidvilasayati, Bodhendra, Brahmendra, Sadananda and others, who authored their own literature on Sankara and Advaita Vedanta.

5.2 SANKARA'S WORKS

Sankara discovered the Highest Truth by churning the knowledge content of *Vedas, Bhagavad-Gita, all the available Upanishads, and Brahmasutra.* His treatises on them with his own interpretations and commentaries, evoking and elucidating their basic message underlying the Advaita philosophy. He was aware of the competing Buddhist doctrine that was popular in those days. He recognized not only the need for clear and convincing exposition of intricate metaphysics, but also the intellectual limitations of the masses. He not only travelled far and wide across the country, but established major centres, known as "Sankar Matts," in the cities of Sringeri, Dwaraka, Badrinath and Puri. He died at an early age of 32.

Adi Sankara is most known for his systematic reviews and commentaries (*Bhasyas*) on ancient Indian texts. Among his commentaries, Sankara's masterpiece work is *Brahmasutrabhasya* (literally, commentary on Brahma Sutra), a fundamental text of the Vedanta school of Hinduism.

His commentaries on ten early Primary Upanishads are also considered authentic by scholars, and these are: *Bhasya* on the Brihadaranyaka Upanishad, the Chandogya Upanishad, the Aitareya Upanishad, the Taittiriya Upanishad, the Kena Upanishad, the Isha Upanishad, the Katha Upanishad, the Mundaka Upanishad, the Prashna Upanishad, and the Mandukya Upanishad. Of these, the commentary on Mandukya, is actually a commentary on Mandukya-Karikas by Gaudapada. Other authentic works of Sankara include commentaries on the Bhagavad Gita (part of his Prasthana Trayi Bhasya). His *Vivarana* (tertiary notes) on the commentary by Vedavyasa on Yoga sutras as well as those on Apastamba Dharma-sutras (*Adhyatama-patala-bhasya*) are accepted by scholars as authentic works of Adi Sankara. Among the *Stotra* (poetic works), the Daksinamurti Stotra, the Bhajagovinda

Stotra, the Sivanandalahari, the Carpata-panjarika, the Visnu-satpadi, the Harimide, the Dasa-Shloka, and the Krishna-sataka are his authentic works.

Sankara also authored *Upadesa-sahasri*, his most important original philosophical work. Of other original '*Prakarana's* monographs, treatise), seventy six works are attributed to Adi Sankara. Modern era Indian scholars such as Belvalkar as well as Upadhyaya accept five and thirty nine works respectively as authentic.

Sankara's stotras considered authentic include those dedicated to Krishna (Vaishnavism) and one to Shiva (Shaivism) – often considered two different sects within Hinduism. Scholars suggest that these stotras are not sectarian, but essentially Advaitic and reach for a unified universal view of Vedanta.

Adi Sankara's commentary on the Brahma Sutras is the oldest surviving. However, in that commentary, he mentions commentaries like those of Dravida, Bhartrprapancha and others which are either lost or yet to be found.

5.3 ULTIMATE REALITY

Adi Sankara systematized the works of preceding philosophers. His system marks a turning point from realism to idealism. His Advaita ("non-dualism") interpretation of the Vedas and Upanishads *(sruti)* postulates the identity of the Self (Atman) and the Whole (Brahman). According to Adi Sankara, the one unchanging entity (Brahman) alone is real, while changing entities do not have absolute existence. The key source texts for this interpretation, as for all schools of Vedanta, are the *Prasthanatraya* mentioned above.

Advaita Vedanta is based on Sastra ("scriptures"), yukti ("reason") and aided by karmas (spiritual practices) at different stages in life, starting from childhood, when learning has to start, the philosophy has to be a way of life. Sankara's primary objective was to understand and explain how moksha is achievable in the present life of the seeker; what it means by liberation which makes one free from the chain of births and deaths, and become a Jivan-Mukta. His philosophical thesis was that jivanmukti is Self-realization, the awareness of Oneness of Self and the Universal Spirit called Brahman, the Supreme Consciousness.

Sankara considered the purity and steadiness of mind achieved in Yoga as only an aid to gaining moksha, but such yogic state of mind cannot in itself give rise to moksha. Only knowledge can lead one to moksha, and to Sankara, that knowledge of Brahman springs only from inquiry into the teachings of the Upanishads. The method of yoga, encouraged in Sankara's teachings includes withdrawal of mind from sense objects as in Patanjali's system, but it is not complete thought suppression, instead it is a "meditative exercise of withdrawal from the particular and identification with the universal, leading to contemplation of oneself as the most universal, namely, Consciousness."

Sankara rejected various yoga systems that suggest complete thought suppression that leads to liberation. He placed great emphasis on the study of the Upanishads, emphasizing them as necessary and sufficient means to gain Self-liberating knowledge. Sankara also emphasized the need for and the role of *Guru* (Acharya, teacher) for such knowledge.

Sankara's Vedanta shows similarities with Mahayana Buddhism; opponents have even accused Sankara of being a "crypto-Buddhist," a qualification which is rejected by the Advaita Vedanta tradition, given the differences between these two schools. According to Sankara, a major difference between Advaita and Mahayana Buddhism are their views on Brahman and Liberation.

5.4 BUDDHISM VS. ADVAITA

Hinduism and Buddhism are closely related. Buddha was a Hindu prince before founding his own path to enlightenment. The relationship between the two is like the relationship between Judaism and Christianity in some ways. Christianity was inspired by the life of a Jew and Buddhism was inspired by the life of a Hindu (though the Buddha rejected Hinduism and did not find it to be the right path for himself).

One of the really stark differences is between *everything* and *nothing*.

Advaita of Hinduism sees the ultimate reality as being all things united as one glorious divinity, Supreme God or Consciousness. Buddhism sees the ultimate reality as *nothingness*. While Hindus gain Moksha and become one with everything in the universe; Buddhists gain Nirvana by detaching from everything until *nothing* remains.

Another big difference is that one of Buddha's fundamental principles is that life is suffering. When we accept that, we want to escape from the world, and so we dedicate ourselves to meditation and breaking the cycle to achieve the nothingness of Nirvana. Advaita of Hinduism, on the other hand, believes that the world is perfect and one must improve and gain knowledge that reveals Consciousness is everything. While Sankara turns to the Vedas, the Upanishads, the Gita, to understand Ultimate Reality, Buddhists do not accept any of the Hindu scriptures.

Buddhism does not worship or follow the Gods. Some don't believe Gods exist and others believe they exist but are not beings worthy of worship, as they are also stuck in the illusion of the world and cannot guide anyone out. It could be said that Buddhism has no Gods while Hinduism has all the Gods! Hinduism, especially Advaita philosophy, Advocates seeing God in every creation.

In day to day practice the most noticeable difference is in rituals. Hinduism has a lot of rituals and proper ways to arrange an altar, proper offerings to make, proper compass directions to face. Buddhism's original forms had none of that.

Recent scholarship states that Sankara's arguments on revelation are about *apta vachana* (sayings of the wise, relying on word, testimony of past or present reliable experts). It is part of his and Advaita Vedanta's epistemological foundation. Advaita Vedanta School considers such testimony valid epistemologically asserting that a human being needs to know numerous facts, and with the limited time and energy available, he can learn only a fraction of those facts and truths directly. Sankara considered the teachings in the Vedas and Upanishads as *apta vachana* and a valid source of knowledge. He suggests the importance of teacher-disciple relationship on combining logic and revelation to attain moksha in his text Upadesha-sara.

5.5 LIBERATION ONLY THROUGH KNOWLEDGE

Traditional Advaita Vedanta centres on the study and correct understanding of the *sruti*, or revealed texts, especially the Upanishads. Correct understanding provides knowledge of the identity of atman and Brahman, which results in liberation. The main texts to be studied are the Upanishads, Brahma Sutras, and Bhagavad Gita. Correct knowledge is obtained by following the four stages:

1. *'Sravana,'* listening to the teachings of the sages,
2. *"Manana" means* contemplating on the teachings repeatedly.
3. *'Nidhidyasana,' analysing what is heard and searching for the truth.*

4. *'Practice' is also needed to "destroy one's tendencies towards sense objects and to purify one's mind and sharpen intellect before real insight can be attained.*

Modern interpretations have recast *anubhava* as "personal experience," in line with Unitarian and Theosophical influences. Yet, *anubhava* does not centre around some sort of "mystical experience," but on the correct knowledge of Brahman. Anantanand Ramadhan quotes several modern interpretations in support of this interpretation, especially Dr. S. Radakrishnan, former president of India, but nevertheless makes clear that *sruti* is the main source of knowledge for Sankara.

Swami Dayananda Saraswati and his disciple, Swami Paripoornananda Saraswati, are advocating, today, the original concepts of Sankara about Advaita Philosophy, without any scope for misunderstanding. They equivocally emphasise that only knowledge is the key to Moksha, and all other forms of worships such as *rituals*, *up-asana*, and *bhakti* are useful only to purify the mind and intellect and makes one eligible to receive the Highest Knowledge. There is a clear distinction between *Knowledge and Anubhava.*

Dayananda Sarasvati explains that interpreting *anubahva* as "experience" may lead to a misunderstanding of Advaita Vedanta, and a mistaken rejection of the study of the scriptures as mere intellectual understanding. Stressing the meaning of *anubhava* as knowledge, Sarasvati argues that liberation comes from knowledge, not from mere experience. Saraswati points out that the experience of the self can never come because consciousness is ever-present, in and through each and every experience, and knowledge of *Atman* and *Brahman* can only be reached by intellect or '*budhi*,' reason', stating that mysticism is a kind of intuitive knowledge, while *buddhi* is the highest means of attaining knowledge.

Brahman (the Absolute) is alone real; this world is unreal; the Jiva or the individual soul is non-different from Brahman. Liberation can be achieved while living, and the person who realises this is called "jeevan-Mukta."

The most incredible fact about Sankara's Advaita philosophy is very close to the latest conclusions reached by modern scientists. What Sankara said about 2000 years ago is true today. His greatest contribution is the theory of knowledge pertaining to non-duality- the oneness of God and the rest of creation. There is no creation, only illusion. His theories are identical to present day uncertainty of particle-wave dual nature of matter, Einstein's Relativity Theories, mass-energy equivalence, and quantum mechanical theories, to name a few. His postulation that Highest Truth must be singular and eternal, and not plural. Its nature is Pure Consciousness, and there can be no second thing that can be real. This is clearly evident from the apparently ever-changing world, expanding universe.

His hypothesis, that only Consciousness is Truth, that exists, and rest of the universe is only an illusory appearance. Scientists have yet to come to this conclusion as they still believe consciousness evolved from matter relying on Darwin's theory of Evolution. Sankara attributed the dual nature of matter to the Subject, while the present scientists are attributing to the objects we see. Scientists, though they claim their ultimate goal is to find the Truth behind the origin of our universe by discovering single Super Force of nature that can explain everything right from the subatomic level to the Cosmos. They have been inventing theories after theories, but facing insurmountable problems. The fact that more and more particles are being discovered at the subatomic level, and dark matter and dark energy are being discovered at the cosmos level, point out that conscious mind of the probing scientists might be the cause of these discoveries.

5.6 DEATH

Adi Sankara is believed to have died at an age of 32, at Kedarnath in the northern Indian state of Uttarakhand, a Hindu pilgrimage site in the Himalayas. Some texts locate his death in alternate locations such as Kanchipuram (Tamil Nadu) and somewhere in the state of Kerala. The most astonishing fact is how he could achieve so-much in such a short span of life. This clearly establishes the theory of karma. The knowledge gained by a person in his previous life will be transferred into present life. In no other way such lives of geniuses can be explained.

6

GOD AND HIS CREATION

6.1 CREATION PROCESS

The creation as described in various Hindu Puranas is meant for common man to create faith in him which is the starting point for acquiring knowledge. The creation described in Upanishads like, Aitareya, Prasna, Svetasvatara, Munduka, and Mandukya Upanishad, and is meant for seekers of highest knowledge. These Upanishads provide an allegorical description of the creation of the universe as well as living beings from one Consciousness. The phenomenal world is originated from this Consciousness which is described as 'Satyam' (eternal), 'Jnanam' (knowledge) and 'Anantham' (All pervading) by Adi Sankaracharya. How this God of Universal Consciousness, without any form, name, or desire created this phenomenal world is beyond the comprehension of ordinary mind. The Upanishads use the word 'Brahman' for the universal consciousness.

Either a single universe or multiple universes are created by Brahman are nothing but figment of imagination or illusion created as if in a dream. Just like we experience all sorts of illusions in dreams, and again it disappears after we wake up. The creation is the spontaneous act of the Creator who is not impelled by any desire or necessity. It is the projection of creator's thoughts.

This illusory world is created, sustained for a while and destroyed, and again this cyclic process repeats. Behind each of these three processes, a presiding deity is imagined. These gods have been named as 'Brahma' the creator,' Vishnu' the sustainer and 'Maheswara' the destroyer. In fact, these three Gods are one and the same. Whenever the universe is created, these three Gods will take up their activities. Brahma is one who can hold this universe within himself, and release during creation process and withdraw during the dissolution. In the unmanifested from he is known as 'Hiranyagarbha, and in the manifested form he is known as 'Virat'. After creation, God Vishnu entered into each and everything, both living and non-living, that has been created. He is known as all-pervading. Maheswara means 'auspicious', the God who is the witness to all these processes. The one individual Brahman (Consciousness) appears threefold through illusion and not in reality. The stages of creation are as follows: 'Iswara' who is of the nature of Pure Consciousness, and, as in dream, he creates 'Hiranyagarbha' with the help of Maya and 'Virat' is created from Hiranyagarbha, the un-manifested form of the world, and from Virat, through the gross elements the manifested world, we see, comprising both living beings and non- living things is formed.

6.2 QUINTUPLICATION (PANCHIKRANAM) PROCESS

The Virat or Brahma created 'Akas' element or Space. From Space, the element 'Air' is created, from Air, the element 'Fire' is created, from Fire, element 'Water' is created, and from Water the element 'Earth' is created. From Earth minerals are formed, from the minerals plant life is created, and from the food man is created. Each of these five elements have their specific characteristics. The element 'Space,' has the characteristic of 'Sound'; the element 'Air' has the characteristics of Sound and Touch; the element 'Fire' has the qualities of Sound, Touch and

Sight; the element 'Water' has the qualities of Sound, Touch, Sight and Taste; finally the element 'Earth' has five qualities, Sound, Touch, Sight, Taste and Smell.

These five subtle elements could not create the universe. The elements have undergone a process known as 'Panchikaranam' or quintuplication. Each of the five elements must be divided into two equal parts (50:50). One of these two parts should be further split into four equal parts (12.5%). Now, the first half comprises the original element, and the second half is filled by the remaining four elements in each of the four quarters as shown in the figure. Thus element 'Akas' will have five constituents parts: that is it comprises of 50% Akas, 12.5% Air, 12, 5% Agni, 12.5% Water, and 12.5% Earth. Likewise all pure elements have undergone quintuplicating process to become compounds. Though each gross element constitutes five elements, it is referred by its own name of the element since it occupies 50%.

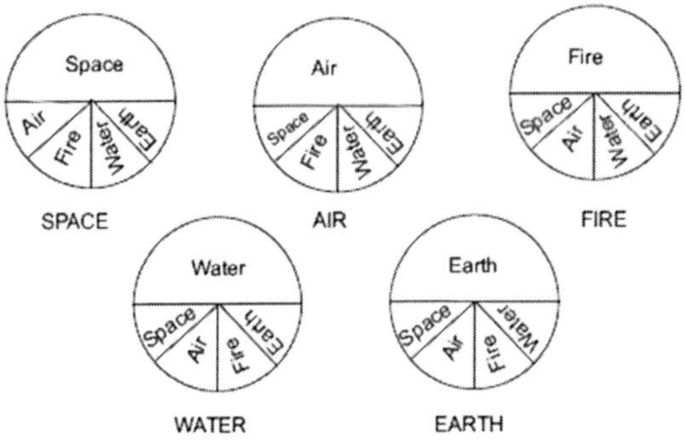

Fig. 6.2 Quantuplication Process

The entire universe or cosmos, known as 'Virat' is created by the admixture of these five gross compounded elements in different proportions. The human body is also created by the same process, except the subtle body consisting of senses, mind and intellect, etc. The macrocosm is represented in miniature form in microcosm of the human being. One individual Brahman or God, appears threefold through illusion and not in reality. These three-fold forms are: the sphere of gods, the sphere pertaining to the physical body, and the sphere of elements. It must be remembered that the Supreme Being reflected in all living beings illumines all the five senses and all five organs of action. We are dead if this energy known as 'Chaitanya' is absent. All inner senses of the subtle body are originated from the Sattva Guna of the subtle elements.

Let us analyze this a bit further. In this world there are basically two things: the observer and the observed. But what makes the difference between the observer and the observed. If the observer has no consciousness he will not be any different from the observed. So, the observer has two parts, one is inert body, and the other is 'Chaitanya' or consciousness. Because of this consciousness, we are able to acquire the knowledge about the external world.

For example, I see a mountain with my eyes. What is seen, namely, the mountain, since it is formed from the five gross element, it said to belong to the sphere of elements. The eye which has seen the object, is an organ of the human body, it is said to belong to the sphere of the physical human body. Even though the eye organ is present some people they cannot see any object because their inner sense organ of sight is defective. This subtle sense of sight cannot function unless it is illumined by the Consciousness. We cannot see the object if it is not illuminated by the sunlight. So, the presiding diety for our vision is known as Sun god. This is how the threefold forms of the creation is described in the Upanishads and Panchikaranam process of creation.

The gross physical body of the human being is formed from the five gross elements, while each of the five senses, stimulated by the respective gods give rise to the knowledge of the objects of the world during waking state, known as 'Visva'.

For example, the organ of hearing belongs to the physical body, whereas what is heard, namely sound, belongs to the sphere of elements, and the sense of hearing belongs to the sphere of gods.

Similarly, the organ of taste, that is Tongue, belongs to the physical human body, what is tasted belongs to the sphere of elements, and sense of taste pertains to the sphere of god known as 'Varun' or Rain god. Likewise, the sense of smell is stimulated by goddess-Earth, the sense of speech belongs to Fire-god. Similarly, the five organs of action, namely, hands, feet, reproduction, and excretion pertain to, respectively, to the spheres of gods, namely, Indra, Vishnu, Prajapati, and god of Death.

In a similar way, the 'Mind' is said to be in the realm of the physical body, whatever is thought is said to belong the world of elements, and Moon god is the presiding deity of the mind. The 'Intellect,' the determining faculty is said to be in realm of the body, whatever is determined belong to the sphere of elements, and god Brhuhaspati is presiding deity of the intellect function. The sense of ego is in the bodily plane, all that concerning which the sense of 'Ego' is exercised belongs to the world of elements, and god Rudra is the presiding deity. The 'Ignorance' belongs to the bodily sphere (causal body), whereas the mutations happening therein are in the sphere of the elements. The supreme God-head is the presiding deity.

There is a similarity between Macrocosm of the universe and the microcosm of the human body. Each is described as having three planes. The sum total of gross bodies of all living beings in this world constitute the gross body of the Lord Brahma, and is known as 'Virat', and corresponds to the waking state of the individual.

Suksma sarira or the subtle body is the combination of the mind, intellect, ego and memory and is known as the transmigrating soul or jiva, which gets separated from the gross body upon death of an individual. The sum total of all the subtle bodies of all the living beings in this world constitute the subtle body of the Creator, and is known as 'Hiranyagarbha'. This corresponds to the dream state of the human being, and the consciousness is known as 'Taijasa'.

Similarly, consciousness associated with deep- sleep state of the individual causal body is known as 'Prajna', and the sum total of all causal bodies is known as 'Iswara', the self of the macrocosm.

6.3 LIFE SPAN OF OUR UNIVERSE

The creation process involves formation of different worlds known as 'Lokas'. The nature and span of this cyclic universe is further explained. The human existence spreads over four Yugas with different spans which repeat themselves.

1. 'Satya-Yuga' (or Krita Yuga):- 17,28,000 Human years
2. 'Treta Yuga':- 12,96,000 Human years
3. 'Dwapara-Yuga':- 8,64,000 Human years
4. 'Kali-Yuga': 4,32,000 Human years (as of 2015, 5,117 years have passed; 4,26,889 years remain). *Kaliyuga* supposed to have started in 3102 B.C.

The total span of the four Yugas together constitute one 'Maha' Yuga. For Lord Brahma, who created this universe, one day or night is equal to thousand Maha Yugas. One full day (Day plus night) for Brahma is 2000 Maha Yugas (8.64 billion years). It is interesting to compare this with the life of sun which has been estimated at 9 billion years. Like this, 100 years is Brahma's life span. This becomes about trillion years. This is the life span of our universe, between its creation and dissolution. During the time of dissolution of the world, a reverse process takes place. The earth gets submerged in water, the water is evaporated by fire, the fire is swallowed by air, and finally, the air merges with akas or space.

It must be mentioned here, that whenever new universe is created, it will have new set of gods: Brahma, Vishnu, and Maheswara.

6.4 DIFFERENT WORLDS

According to Hindu scriptures, God Brahma has created fourteen worlds, seven above the earth and seven below; and different category of living being, need not be of human form, populate these worlds depending on their karmas. The worlds are named as "Lokas": Earth is known as *Bhuloka* higher above this are *Bhuvar loka*, *Svaharloka*, *Maharloka*, *Janaloka*, *Tapohloka* and *Satyaloka.* More evolved souls occupy these higher lokas in that order. Similarly lower souls go to lokas that are below this earth or Bhuloka. They are, in the order of descending, are: *Atala*, *Vitala, Sutala*, *Talatala*, *Rasatala*, *Mahatala* and *Patala* where the worst form of demons live.

On Earth, there are about 8.4 million living species, without one resembling the other. These are classified into four groups: 'Svedaja' those creatures born of sweat; 'Udbija' those sprout from earth, like plants, which comprise of different forms of flora; 'Andaja' those species born out of eggs; birds, reptiles, etc.; 'Jarayuja' those mammalian species born out of womb which include human beings. Each of these species population comprises of 2.1 million.

In the case of human beings, they are further classification into three groups based on their behavioural characteristic known as 'Gunas'. People of god nature exhibiting characteristics such as such love, compassion and interested in knowing about their true nature are known as 'Sattivik' type; those who are interested in worldly pursuits and sense gratification are known as 'Rajasic' type; and those who exhibit wicked and cruel characteristics are known as 'Tamasic' type. This can be stated in a simple way like this: the man whose mind is calm is known to possess Sattvik characteristics, the man whose mind is agitated is said to possess Rajasic characteristics, and the man whose mind is clouded by delusions is characterised as Tamasik.

The human beings undergo changes in their characteristics as they age, and finally what decides his future form of birth is the characteristics he inculcated at the time of his death. So, the classification of the souls is done based on the characteristics and desires of an individual at the time of his death. For example, if a man dies in an accident, he might take birth as human being on earth or born in another world depending on his characteristics and desires at he time of his death.

The people are divided by the nature of combination of these basic characteristics they possess. For example, Adhama Sattviki (lowest among good), Atyanta Tamas (highly bad), Rajas Sattviki (mixed qualities of good and bad), Atyanta Tamasi (worst among the cruel), etc. Depending on classification like this, the souls occupy the fourteen worlds. It is said only a person who is highly evolved possessing Sattvik Guna will be inclined towards knowing about himself, the external world and God. Thus his spiritual journey to higher worlds or lokas starts.

A person, depending on his spiritual progress, he ascends to the higher worlds. For example, the average spiritual level of a person on earth might be 20 to 30 percent. When a person's spiritual knowledge raises to 50 percent, he might ascend to the next higher loka, Bhuvar loka; and a person with 70 percent spiritual progress ascend to Svaharuvar Loka or Swarga loka as it is called. This Swarga loka is sometimes referred as heaven, and a person who reaches here enjoys abundance of happiness. However, after exhausting his positive karmas, he once again reincarnates a body and takes birth on earth. As the person's spiritual level increases further to 80 percent, he ascends to Mahar Loka, similarly a person with 85 percent goes to Jana Loka, with 90 percent level of spiritual progress, Tapo Loka, and with 95 percent he ascends to Satya Loka or Brahma Loka as it is called. The person who ascends to this world, shall not be reborn, but stays there for a very long period, and finally he acquires the Self-knowledge and merges with the supreme Self at the time of dissolution of the world. When a person acquires 100 percent spiritual level by gaining Self-knowledge, before death, there is no departure of his subtle body or soul and he no more takes birth, since he merges with the Supreme at the time of death itself.

On the other hand, say, a person commits suicide, he will become a ghost because they had lot of unfulfilled desires and attachments before death, and go to the lower worlds below earth. The dead occupies different lower worlds depending on their characteristics at the time of their death.

6.5 DIFFERENT GODS

Since the illusory nature of the universe, and the formless God is difficult to grasp by a common man, God can be imagined in any form and name for worship. To discipline the society, it is necessary to inculcate the fear of god, who is superior to human beings, in the minds of people right from their childhood. So the concept of god, sitting in the heaven, rewarding the virtuous and punishing the wicked has been created. Everything we see or experience in this is described as gods or goddesses in Hindu scriptures. For example, the rain is referred as rain god, wind as wind god, similar, the god of fire, the goddess of knowledge (Saraswati), the goddess of bestowing wealth (Lakshmi), and god of removal of obstacles (Ganesh) and so on. This concept, in fact, is very good in view of protecting and safeguarding the health of our planet, because most of the animals and plants are regarded as gods or goddesses.

In every one's mind, one day or other a question arises, who is God and what is his form? Why he created such a vast universe to create life on a small planet like earth? Different religions had given different definitions of God.

Some religions assume God stays in heaven and created this universe. If this is so, God must be human-like with desires and feelings, liking and disliking, blessing those who praise him and worship, and punishing the wicked. If this were true why God had to create such a vast universe? If we assume spherical universe, it will have a radius of 14 billion light years. The life exists only on earth, and scientists could not find anywhere else so far. Yet, some other religions imagine God is like an extraordinary human being with four or eight hands, and one weapon in each hand. The all powerful God who created this vast universe, why does he require weapons? This can be interpreted to indicate two aspects of God. One is to show God is superior to ordinary souls, and secondly, weapon in each hand are symbolic to the elimination of bad qualities in human beings such as pride, desires, ego, etc. Analysing like this, one comes to the conclusion, that God must be formless, without name, and he did not create this universe. He does not interfere with day to day human affairs. He does not shower boons and punish the wicked. He is of the nature of pure Consciousness that energises each one of us.

The process of creation of the universe is said to have started by the creator, the Supreme God with the help of 'Maya'. This Maya has the following characteristics. They are known as Sattva, Rajas, and Tamas as explained already. As long as these three Gunas of nature are in equilibrium, there is no creation. Once the equilibrium is disturbed, the creation process begins. In addition, Maya has two more characteristics, namely, *Vikshepa Sakti* and *Avarana Sakti.* Vikshepa Sakti means the power of projection. The illusory world is a projection. Avarana Sakti means the power to conceal, or veiling power. That is it make things appear or disappear, and makes us feel we are limited beings. The Maya can be classified as positive or negative, and passive or dynamic. The appearance of sky as blue, and appearance of a rainbow are examples of passive Maya. Mistaking a rope for a snake and running for life is an example of dynamic Maya.

6.6 NATURE OF GOD

The human body can be classified into three parts: Gross body, the subtle body and the Causal body. Gross body and subtle body have been explained. The nature of the Causal body is very difficult to explain and so it is indefinable. It is enveloped by Ignorance (or Ajnana). The ignorance comprises of Malam (impurities in the mind), Vikshepa Sakti (Projecting power) and Avarana (Concealing power).

The world is not real, as it has been established in the earlier chapter. Our universe, as we can imagine, comprises of only four things: space, time, living beings and no-living matter. Out of these, space, time and matter can expand and contract. That is they are subjected to change. Also living beings, including human beings undergo change in size right from the time of birth. It must be noted, all that is created has name and form. Anything that has name and form will become non-existent one day. That is death is inevitable to all that is created. The criteria applied to define God is, that it must not undergo any change or decay, and He must be eternal. If we apply these criteria to God, assumed to be the creator of this universe, if he has name and form he will be non-existent one day. A non-eternal being obviously cannot be the cause of this universe. God has been defined as eternal, knowledge and omnipresent. That is stated as *Satyam (eternal), Jnanam (knowledge) and Anantham (all pervading).*

We face another question? Can eternal god create anything eternal? Whatever we see, and what extent we can imagine, we do not see anything eternal. We see the stars taking birth, existing for a few million or billion years and dying. From the dust of the dead stars new stars are born. These stars form into galaxies and cluster of galaxies, planets, etc. If there is one more eternal that is created, then there must another cause to create two eternal things. It can logically be concluded that two eternal things cannot coexist. From this we can conclude that God alone is eternal.

Let assume for a moment that God has created this universe. Now the question is whether God resides outside the universe or inside the universe? For example, I created the image of Mahatma Gandhi from a rock by sculpting. Without doubt the image is outside me; I and the sculpture created by me are different. So, the God must lie outside the universe. But according to science there is nothing outside the universe. There is no meaning talking about what is outside the universe. This brings us to the fact that if God has created the universe the God and Universe must be one and the same. Again, by the earlier logic, if one is real the other must be an illusion. We come to the conclusion that world must be an illusion and has no bearing or support for its existence.

Again, if God has created this universe, he must have desired to do so. We have proved that the origin of the desire is ignorance. This leads to the conclusion that God is ignorant being which cannot be true. Analysing like this it can be established that God is a Pure Consciousness without name or form, and all pervading; he has no wishes or desires to perform or do something to please who prays for him, and punish the sinners. He has no attributes such as liking or disliking.

If one imagines God as the cause for the universe and the universe is the effect. If we accept this we have to conclude that there must be another cause to create God. This is not tenable.

There are four types of cause and effect situations that one can imagine.

First one is the example of milk turning into curds. Here the milk, the cause, has undergone a chemical change, and so curds is the effect. The properties of the curd are entirely different from the milk.

The second type of cause-effect relation can be sited as, the pot is made from clay. Here pot is the effect and clay is the cause. The material content of both the clay and pot is same, except probably the pot is baked under fire and it appears little strong. The third cause-effect is the waves we see on the surface of the sea. Here sea is the cause and waves are the effect. But if you touch the waves it is water which is same as that of sea.

The fourth type of cause and effect is mistaking a rope to be a snake when the light is dim. Here the person who sees the rope lying on the road and mistakes for snake, he is actually afraid and starts sweating, and decides to run away. Instead, had he decides to focus a light and verify, he would have found the truth. His fear is mainly due to ignorance. Adi Sankara repeatedly quotes this example of cause- effect relation as that of between man and the world. The world appears as real because of one's ignorance. Once the ignorance is removed with right knowledge, the ignorance disappears.

This three-fold appearance (in the shape of creation, continuance and destruction of the universe) in the Self has been declared (by the wise) as baseless. One must know the threefold existence (in the shape of the perceiver, the perceived, and the act of perception) being a product of three Gunas, as brought out by Maya (the deluding potency of the Self). One who comes to know (what is meant by) this ripeness of Jnana, as presented in the scriptures, would neither extol nor revile any one, and move about in the world (free from partiality and prejudice) as the sun.

Realising this world as having a beginning and an end, and therefore unreal by means of perception, inference based on the authority of the scriptures and one's own direct experience, one would move in this world unattached. There is a quotation on this from Ashta Vakra Gita by Swami Chinmayananda.

"There is nothing real or unreal in this world. It is the mind that takes something for real or unreal. It is the mind that is responsible for illusions or delusions."

7

THE THEORY OF KARMA

7.1 EVOLUTION OF PERSONALITY

Close look at the Darwin's theory of evolution of life on earth, one finds that life evolved from single-celled creatures to multi-cellular bacteria, fish, reptiles, birds, mammals and finally man evolved from monkey. In other words it is the progressive development of organizational complexity. If this theory were right, human beings evolved from monkeys, like all other animals, must have evolved to the same degree. But we observe one man is mean, and selfish, while the other is magnanimous and altruistic; one is wicked while another is virtuous. These qualities were observed right from the childhood. One is intelligent right from the age two, while another child is dull. Such large scale personality differences are uncommon in the animal kingdom. Also the concept how consciousness evolved from lifeless matter is still a conundrum.

Therefore it is necessary to divide the evolution of human personality into two kinds: one that majority of people evolved based on the five senses, namely, sight, hearing, touch, smell and taste. They interact with the external environment using these five senses to make their progress. We can say, most of us, are five-sensory human beings with survival as the primary goal. Man has been utilizing the gifted intelligence to acquire, by all means, control over the environment for their physical comforts, and rule over people within it. This goal enabled him to survive harsh environment populated by more powerful and strong wild animals. This power can be called as the 'External Power' as mentioned by Gary Zukav. The competition for this external power is mainly responsible for wars around the world, and dividing countries into various economic jones. The currency based GDP has become symbol of progress of the nations. However, such progress, in the long run, brings only pain and destruction.

When we observe closely we find another type of evolution among the human beings who can be called great Souls born around the world with 'Internal Power'. For example, the seven Indian Rishis, Buddha, Jesus, Prophet Mohamed, Mahatma Gandhi, to name a few, can be called as evolved Souls. They had seen the world differently. Their influence on society was so great, millions of people have become their followers. They have been transformed from the five- sensory humans with greed for External Power into evolved souls with Internal Power.

Greed, anger, fear, hatred, vengeance, sorrow, shame, regret, indifference and cynicism are the characteristics of the five-sensory people with desire for external power, while love, compassion, and wisdom are the characteristics of the evolved souls with internal power. One can observe the difference between the two types of human beings lies in their energy levels of their souls or self. As the energy of a person's consciousness increase, the quality of his internal power reflects in clarity in their thinking, speech and deeds and humbleness, forgiveness and love for humanity and nature, These qualities of the evolved person touches more and more people around him who seek his company for guiding their lives.

The energy of the soul is not a passive or a theoretical entity that occupies a space in one's chest cavity; it is positive, purposeful force at the core of each personality.

The question arise how the human beings with internal power evolved? They did not appear suddenly on this planet. These souls evolved gradually, passing through many lives and gradually increasing the energy of their souls.

In fact, the journey of the soul stops when it gains its full energy, and its migration or incarnation ends. Such a soul will not take birth again. Therefore the question is how the energy of the soul increases? It is simple; by good nature and knowledge. The personality and its body are temporary aspects of the soul. When they have served their function at the end of their life, the soul releases them and its journey continues, and incarnates another body. The conflicts that arise during man's life are directly proportional to the distance at which the energy of the personality exists separately from its soul. The law of karma follows the third law of motion that governs the balance of energy within our evolutionary system. A person who intends hatred to others experiences hatred from others. The person who intends love for others, experiences love from others. Each personality is different because the configuration of the energy of the soul that was responsible for the personality. Every negative action drains energy of the soul, while good actions increases the energy of the soul.

When a personality becomes successful in getting rid of his greed for the external power, anger and jealousy, it aligns with its soul that is full of love and compassion, reflecting the energy of the soul. It must be remembered that a fully evolved soul is incapable of harming another.

The evolution towards internal power affects not only one personality, but also the entire humanity. The journey of the soul to its wholeness requires one must look honestly, openly and with courage into oneself, into the dynamics of the energy that lie behind its evolution. Therefore the knowledge of the Self is the key for the evolution of the soul and to put an end to its journey.

7.2 DESTINY AND KARMA

"Every living being is born alone and dies alone by itself. Alone it enjoys the fruit of its good deeds and alone does it reap the consequences of its misdeeds"- Karma literally means the actions performed by an individual not only in this life, but also in the previous lives. If a person is wealthy, know it is because of his good karmas in the previous lives; if a man is poor or born as a handicapped child, know it is because of his past karmas; similarly, if a man is altruist, knowledgeable and wise, know it is because of his past good karmas.

The destiny, we call, is nothing but the cumulative result of our own actions, we might have done during our past lives that are forgotten, and not accessible. But the law of karma is that the reaction to our action will bear fruit either in this present life, or in our future lives. The laws of karma and the laws of nature were created when the universe was created. For, example, ice is cold, and fire will be hot are the laws of nature, as we know, and are applicable everywhere in the universe. But the laws of karma, though universal, are applicable to only individuals. For example, I kill a person, out of enmity, in this life. The agony and suffering inflicted on the victim will reflect back on me either in the present life or next life, making me suffer similar pain and agony. Likewise, there will be equal reaction for every action.

All actions that we perform bear fruit one day or other, however, all consequences are neither apparent nor predictable. For example, a person saved money, over a period, and with that he purchased his dream car. With this action, not only he is happy, but, probably, entire family is happy. Here the action and its consequences are apparent. Now let us say, after a year or two, his young son takes the car out and makes an accident and dies. This accident is an unexpected consequence, the man might think, had I not bought the car, I would not have lost my son. In fact, the death of his son, and his action of buying a car have no relation. His son's death is due to the result of his action in his previous life. Therefore, all family members, though living under the same roof, the destiny of each one will be different. Each soul has its own journey.

7.3 KARMAS - CLASSIFICATION

Any action done with a desire or motive leaves in our mind subtle impressions, known as 'Samskaras', which bring about consequences in the present or future lives. The theory of '**Karma**' is common to many oriental religions. In its most popular form it states that there is a universal accounting system in which each individual must experience the consequences of all his actions (Karmas); good actions bring good results and bad actions inevitably result in suffering to the one who does them. The theory also states that the consequences of actions (also known as Karmas) need not necessarily be experienced in the present life, they can be carried over into future lives. Because of this, several sub-divisions of Karma have been postulated. The following classification, which was used by Sri Ramana Maharshi, is common to many Hindu schools of thought.

'Sanchita Karma' are the store of Karmic debts accumulated from previous births. 'Prarabdha' Karma' are that part of one's Sanchita Karma which must be worked out in the present life. Because the law of Karma implies determinism in human activities, Prarabdha is often translated as destiny. 'Agami Karma' are the new Karmas accumulated in the present lifetime which is carried forward into future lives. Sri Ramana Maharshi accepted the validity of the laws of Karma but said that they were only applicable as long as a person imagined that he was separate from the Self.

There are three kinds of Prarabdha karma: *Ichha* (personally desired), *Anichha* (without desire) and *Parechha* (due to others' desire). For a self-realized person, there is no Ichha-Prarabdha but the two others, Anichha and Parechha, remain, which he has to be undergone by one and all.

In Vedantic literature, there is a beautiful analogy. The bowman has already sent an arrow and it has left his hands. He cannot recall it. He is about to shoot another arrow. The bundle of arrows in the quiver on his back symbolises the *sanchita*; the arrow he has shot is *prarabdha;* and the arrow which he is about to shoot from his bow is *agami*. Of these, he has perfect control over the sanchita and the agami, but he must surely face his prarabdha. The past which has begun to take effect in the present life, one has to experience.

The karmas we do, with our free will, in the present life will get added to the accumulated karmas (Sanchita Karmas), and will bear fruit in future lives, or sometimes in the future of present life. However, for man who gained Self-knowledge, since he knows the root cause, he bears the fruits of Prarabdha karma smilingly.

According to Hinduism, after we die, we take birth incarnating new body, but the old Sankara, the accumulated karmas carried by the subtle body continue as this is the law of karma. Karma and rebirth are the two great pillars of Hinduism. He who does not believe in these two great truths cannot grasp the essence of the religion. The Newton's third law 'For every force, there will be equal reaction' seems to be relevant in man's personal life too. Whatever action or karma we do it bears some fruit that in our present life or future lives. The result of action cannot be avoided unless we gain complete knowledge about the 'Law of Karma'.

What many call destiny is nothing but actions we did, out of our own free will, in our past lives. In our present life, we enjoy ourselves or suffer for the actions we did in our past lives. Similarly, what actions we perform, in our present life, out of our free- will, one has to bear its consequences in the next life or future lives. Therefore our goal, in life, is to play the difficult game well, with judicious use of free will, and emerge winners. Nothing can be more rewarding and satisfying than this.

One can overcome pain and sorrow, if he knows the cause for sorrow, pain, suffering and death. The phenomenon of death sets the human mind to think deeply. All philosophies sprang up from the phenomenon of death. Philosophy, in a sense, is really the study of death. The highest philosophy in India starts with the subject of death in scriptures like Bhagavad-Gita, Katha Upanishad and Chandogya Upanishad. The goal in life is to know the Truth, the Eternal God or Brahman. Death is nothing but the change of body. The soul or 'jiva' as it is called, throws off its body like a used garment. Human life is about getting purged and perfected in order to attain the final bliss. This takes place through myriads of births. According to Hinduism, life is one continuous, never-ending process. All change is only change of environment and embodiment.

7.4 LAW OF KARMA

The theory of karma, according to Indian Scriptures, says that we are born of karma, we live by karma and we die by karma. Karma simply means different actions. We are born to our parents. They desired to have a child and performed karma, and as a result we are born. Ever since we are born we keep doing something or other to survive and involve in different activities. We drink milk, eat food, play and learn and grow. We learn some skill, we take up employment to earn our livelihood, and get married, and the story repeats. We become old and die, carrying with us the accumulated karmas, to be born again.

When we introspect, sometimes, we will be perplexed. Why we are born to these particular parents, particular place or particular country? Why I did not take birth in a richer country? Why I was born to these poor parents? Why I am born with a defect? Why others are more intelligent than me? Why I am suffering? Why I am not happy? These questions can be answered only when we are convinced about past lives and future rebirths. We observe, children born to the same parents are differently abled in their walks of life. Even twins do not share all the qualities as they grow up. They will follow different ways of life. All these observations point to one thing; what we are now, because of what actions or karmas we performed in our previous lives. For every action there will be a reaction. Let us explore this journey of the soul a little further.

Suppose someone was born on 29th June 1944. Does this mean he was not there on 28th June 1944? No, he was there in his mother's womb for nine months. Where was he before that? He was with his father in the form of semen. Where was he before that? He was in the form of food his father was taking, that became semen. Where from the food came? The food came from trees. Where from trees came? We know, for a tree to grow five elements are needed: earth, water, sunlight, air and space. Another way of realising is the fact we are all born out of food. We survive by eating food, our body grows in size by eating food, and when we die we are buried or burnt so that we merge with food or five elements. So the seed of life or jiva, from the five elements, enters through the rain, and results in the food, which in turn results in man's semen and new life process starts. Thus the journey of the soul or jiva continues life after life.

We do not know how and when we are going to die. This again is due to karmas in our previous lives. One might die of a disease after suffering many years. Another might die in a road accident. Yet another might be killed by his enemy. The doubtless fact is that we are going to die one day. However, we do not know when, where and how? We can imagine the five elements of nature, combine with each other in different ways, and this process known as 'quintuplication' is responsible for the creation of the world we see, including all living beings and non-living things.

Thus the karmas bind us to the cycle of birth and death which will continue until we learn how to break away from this cycle and get liberated and attain "Moksha." This moksha is eternal and is a state of blissful awareness. Scriptures say the goal of human life is to attain this state. Interesting fact is that this "Bliss" state has to be achieved before our death. The happiness, which all living beings struggle to gain by all materialistic means is however a temporary phenomenon. But Bliss is eternal and can be achieved while we are alive. The chain of repeated births bearing all miseries, diseases, old age and death, can be avoided by acquiring Self-knowledge. Once a man realises this knowledge, his Sanchita karmas and Agami karmas will be nullified instantly.

7.5 ONLY KNOWLEDGE IS IMPORTANT

This state of Bliss has been quantified in the scriptures. If one calls the happiness of a strong, powerful, healthiest, and wealthiest person on this planet as one unit, the person who enjoys Bliss is more than billion times. This is the attraction that drives few, if not many, to enjoy this state before death and liberation thereafter. There were great many people who achieved and there is a lot to learn from them, and also the means to achieve has been well documented. Knowledge is the only means to enjoy bliss, and is called the "Highest Truth" or eternal "knowledge." People who lack this knowledge are always fearful of disease, old age and death. One must understand that all these human sufferings is due to ignorance that can be removed only by knowledge.

This liberation or moksha cannot be gained by good deeds, charity, fasting or prayers, or meditation, etc. since these are all actions in one form or other. All actions are limited in nature and so they cannot result in the Bliss which is eternal. So, eternal thing can be gained only by Self-knowledge that is eternal. If the individual beings are themselves a product of karma and ignorance, how can actions performed by them lead to final liberation?

This highest knowledge is knowing about one's true nature, which is but Pure Consciousness. The knowledge of science, as we know, is about the objective world; it involves the study of the physical, chemical or biological phenomena taking place in the world around us. This knowledge is hidden in everything we observe or see. The knowledge of photosynthesis as how to convert solar energy into food is hidden in the leaf of a tree or a plant. The knowledge of a tree, as how high it grows, what fruit it bears, etc. are hidden in the seed. The knowledge of nuclear energy is hidden in an atom. The knowledge about a human being is hidden in his genes. This kind of knowledge is known as perceptive knowledge, and does not lead to liberation or moksha. For moksha, we need subjective knowledge, knowledge about oneself. These two are quiet opposite.

The actions or karmas we perform in our day to day life are limited in nature. Bigger is the desire for the materialistic goal, bigger actions are required to be performed. More money has to be earned to gain more materialistic comforts. We have to expend more energy and time to gain certain comforts in life. By this logic we have to perform unlimited actions to achieve unlimited happiness or freedom. We immediately try to conclude that not doing any karmas is the solution. This is not true. There was a king by name Janaka, who lived long ago, who realised this highest knowledge, and ruled the kingdom there after. He was called Raja Rishi. Also the story of Rama, the God incarnate, leant this knowledge at a very young age of 16, from his guru sage Vasishta, there after he got married to the daughter of King Janaka and faced lot of ordeals in life and at the end ruled the kingdom.

Yet another instance is the preaching of Lord Krishna, as depicted in Bhagavad-Gita, advises Arjun to fight with his cousins, in the great epic war, Mahabharata, to establish Dharma, and not for any gain. A karma performed for the sake of protecting Dharma, and not for any materialistic gains, after the knowledge dawns, is not binding on the person. The mind goes out to do karma in this materialistic world, while to acquire the highest knowledge the mind must make inward journey. Karma performed, after gaining knowledge is considered as non-action (Akarma). In this context, some learned men say that Jnana (knowledge) and karma (action) are 180 degrees opposite.

We are compelled into action because of desires. When one desire is accomplished another desire crops up. If the desire is not fulfilled it leads to frustration and anger. Even if the desire is fulfilled, the happiness does not last long. So another desire arises in the mind. Likewise desires will be cropping up one after another. The result of these desires and subsequent actions will bring happiness or misery alternately in a sequence. Thus, it is the mind which is the doer of our actions, not the body. In other words, if our mind is not involved in our actions, they cannot be considered as binding actions. Therefore, the actions performed without any expectation, or desire for fruits of action, will not be binding the man. They do not form part of either Sanchita, Prarabdha or Agami karmas.

7.6 KARMA AND DHARMA

It is not possible to lead a life without doing actions or karmas. There are other types of karmas or actions we perform during our life time. The society has long recognised that everyone is born free. However, he cannot be a law unto himself. If one has freedom and rights, he has also responsibilities and duties towards his family and society. An ordered society is possible only when each citizen who make up the society are aware of their duties and put them into practice. An individual while enjoying freedom, should not do anything that harms another individual or the society at large. Keeping this in mind, ancient Vedic Scholars postulated *Dharma* which allows certain actions while prohibiting certain others. The principle of Dharma is nothing but prescription of the righteous path for the individual's duty towards his family, society and also that path must enable him to reach the goal of human life before his death. Therefore, the human actions have been classified into five categories: 'Nitya', 'Nymittika', 'Kamya', 'Nisshiddha' and 'Prayachitta'.

'Nitya' karmas are those which we do from the time we wake up early in the morning until the time we go to bed. These include our daily karmas, we have to perform while interacting with the external world. After taking bath, one must express gratitude to his parents, to the sun god, the goddess earth, studying scriptures, prayer, etc. For example, a person does not exist on this planet without his parents, without the energy received from the Sun there is no life, and without this planet Earth there is no shelter for all of us. Therefore this quality of expressing gratitude to them only distinguishes man from an animal.

Similarly, for food production, the five elements of nature are essential, these are referred as gods and goddesses. For example, rain god, wind god, fire god, etc. It is the duty of every one to express gratitude to these gods and goddesses for providing us food.

'Nymittika' karmas are dutiful karmas or actions. These are obligatory duties. These include conducting rituals and ceremonies on the occasion of birth, marriage or death of a member in the family. Ancestor-worship is one of the fundamental doctrines of Hinduism. There are three stages in the ancestral life viz., father, grandfather and great grandfather, and mother, grandmother and great grandmother. One has to offer Shraddha, Tarpana and other religious rites on specified day every year to the departed souls of parents, and grandparents. Not obliging such duties do great harm to their ancestors and themselves and also amounts to sin for the person.

'Kamya' karmas are those performed to fulfil once desires, such as taking up a profession to earn one's livelihood. One must be duty bound to perform entrusted work efficiently and satisfactorily. Everyone in this world has aspirations to achieve certain goals he sets for himself. He wishes for studies, good job, good wife, decent house, children, etc. The karmas one does to fulfil such desires are called Kamya Karmas. Sometimes, the time or conditions will not be favourable to achieve his desires. To remove the obstacles he might do special Poojas, Yagas or Yagnas. There is also another category of karmas that come under Kamya karma. This woman is my wife, this child is mine, and I have to take care of them. This country is mine I have to work for my country. These are all actions one has to perform as unavoidable, and all dutiful actions fall under Kamya karmas.

'Nishiddha' karmas are the karmas or actions which are prohibited by the scriptures. Because they are against moral values or promulgated legal law. Prohibited karmas are dictated by law and moral code of conduct and values. Nishiddha karmas are harmful to the man and the society at large. For example, stealing other's goods or hurting others physically or mentally, using abusive language against someone, practicing criminal acts or killing fellow citizen, etc. In Hindu societies marriages are for life and divorces are rare and not liked by the society. Similarly immoral acts such as extramarital affairs are prohibited. These prohibited acts are not conducive for spiritual growth of a person. In fact such acts bind a man for repeated births with bad consequences. The feelings of 'I, me, and mine' is the root cause for greed and corruption in the society. Unless they are kept under check it is not possible for the society to progress. In simple, any action by the citizen of the society that harms another citizen or society at large are prohibited actions.

A person not doing his duty also amounts to a bad karma. For example, one has to take care of his parents during their old age. So, not doing such duties to his family and parents attracts sin and such a person does not enjoy any respect in the society.

'Prayachitta' karmas are those punishments one imposes on himself. For example, a person unknowingly hurts or causes physical injury to another person; he feels guilty and wants to punish himself. Christians go to Church and confess; Hindus go to temple and go round the temple, say, hundred times. Some walk on fire, some slap themselves. Shia Muslims, beat with chains around their chest. A person, while reversing his car, killed his own 3 year old son. One can imagine the agony suffered by him and his wife. They go on pilgrimage, take bath in holy rivers, etc. These are self-imposed punishments and are called Prayachitta karmas.

In our daily life many things or actions take place over which we have no control. We have no control on the choice of parents, country or place of birth, kind of body with physical defect or handsome face. Similarly, we have no control over the functioning of our physical body. The organs like our heart, lungs, kidneys and liver function by themselves, without any effort by us. The hormone glands, blood circulation, immune system, digestive system, body temperature control system, excretion system, etc. function without rest. This raises a question; whether we are masters of our own lives or guided by some unknown force.

Each one of us has "free will" and choice with regard to doing karmas. I may decide to do certain karma immediately, or postpone it by few days or might decide not to do at all. This free will has to be used judiciously otherwise the karmas will bind us to the cycle of birth and death. Our thoughts, speech and actions must be truthful and must be in tune with Dharma with good intentions, and must be useful to the society at large. Such actions performed without expecting anything in return, will not bind us. As a law, all karmas, we do will bring about some results, some of which are to our liking and others are imposed against our liking.

It is interesting to analyse what drives to do karmas. Let us assume we confine a billionaire to a house and he has everything he desires at his command, but he cannot go out of his house. Can such a man be happy? No, not at all. He cannot sit idle wasting time. He wants to invest and make more money or start a new business. This desire to do something comes from the void in the mind which drives him lazy and crave for something which sometimes he cannot define. What causes this void is ignorance or lack of right knowledge. So the root cause of action or karma is ignorance in the mind. When the highest knowledge dawns in the mind of a person, he is not compelled to do karma. He is happy without doing any work. But he does not become lazy as many expect. He does the karmas what is expected of him. He performs his duties to his family or work place. But now his attitude will be totally different. No karmas will bind him. He enjoys bliss wherever he goes. He is no more interested in the fruits or outcome his actions or karmas. The aim of this book is to elaborate as what this highest knowledge and how one can acquire. At the end, we realise that we are bound by neither action nor destiny, as everything is just a stage play. Only thing is, we have to perform our role well. Therefore the goal of life is to earn rightfully, fulfil rightful desires so that at the end they must lead person to enjoy unlimited happiness and liberation at the end. That is the purpose of life of an individual, and religion and its scriptures are meant to guide man as how to live a life and reach the goal.

The Hindu scriptures prescribe four-fold guidelines as how to lead a life and how to reach one's goal in life. These are called, *Dharma, Artha*, *Kama* and *Moksh*a. The middle two, namely Kama and Artha, are meant to guide man how to lead a life and earn his livelihood, and fulfil his desires by following Dharma. This process of earning by rightful or virtuous means to fulfil one's desires is known as Ardha. The desires that propel man to do actions is known as Kama. These actions, finally must help and aid him to gain self-knowledge, which is his goal for life, and is known as Moksha.

7.7 PROCESS OF DEATH AND KARMA

The departure of the individual soul, at the time of death, for different people who try to reach God by Karma, Upasana or Jnana have been depicted in the Brhmasutras and as described by Sage Vasishta are presented below:

When an ordinary person dies, first the senses lose their activity, followed by absence of breathing ability, heart fails to function and finally brain function ceases. The subtle body comprising of mind, intellect, ego and memory, leaves the body carrying all the knowledge acquired in the present life as well as previous lives, and forms the seed for next life. This is sometimes referred as Jiva leaving the body. It departs the physical body through one of the openings like eyes, nose, ears, mouth, etc. In accordance with his Sanchita and Agami karmas, he takes birth again after prescribes stay in one of the Lokas, other than Satya Loka. For example, a man who does not believe in God, and resorts to all types of bad karmas might take birth in the lower worlds.

Those who worship God using symbols, idols with names and forms (Saguna-Upasana), do not go to Brahma Loka, but they are sure to be born on earth again. The Jiva departs the physical body through one of the organs, eyes, ears, nose, etc. at the time of death. He will take birth again on earth as a human being and gets one more chance to gain self-knowledge.

One who meditates on God without using any symbols (Nirguna –Upasana) goes to Brahma Loka or Satya Loka and does not come back to earth again. For the person who meditates on God or Brahman without using any symbols or idols, his Jiva, from the heart, departs through the Subhuman Nadi through the skull after death. The jiva or soul reaches the deities of Fire, Air, the Sun, and Moon, the world of Varuna, world of Indra, Prajapathi, and finally the world of Brahma. On the dissolution of Brahma Loka, all the souls along with its ruler, attain the supreme Brahman, having realised the Self-knowledge by that time.

The person who has gained the Self-knowledge, there will no departure at all for the Jiva. The subtle body merges with gross body at the time of death itself. He attains the absolute Brahman and will not take birth at all. This departure of jiva depends on the condition of the individual at the time of death, and the knowledge he gained. This again depends the mind of the individual. Therefore understanding the working of the mind is very important.

8

MIND IS EVERYTHING

8.1 FUNCTIONS OF MIND

Mind is everything: Our genes, our health, our knowledge, our wealth, our desires and worries, our pleasures and pains, and finally our death are linked to our mind. In fact our mind controls all bodily functions like breathing, heartbeat, body temperature, blood sugar, our actions, our behaviour, our goals, our friends and our relationships, our character and conduct.

Our genes configure our body, its health and diseases; the brain organises our genes, and our knowledge organises our brains. The mind only acquires knowledge. It is important to understand this quote: "Knowledge shapes our thoughts, thoughts shape our attitude, our attitude shapes our behaviour, and our behaviour shapes our destiny."

Therefore understanding mind is paramount important. Most of us engaged in worldly affairs day in and day out and ignore the need to understand our own mind. Knowing all about the world seems wasting time without understanding about ourselves. But what is mind? What are its functions? Does it exist at all?

The mind can be defined as a set of cognitive faculties that enable thinking, judgment, memory and the ego consciousness. It is observed that other life forms also possess mind except there are differences in the degree of development of the faculties. It is called as 'mind' when we are thinking of something; it is called 'intellect' when we are deciding between choices; it is called 'memory' when we are storing information or retrieving it, and it is called 'ego' when we identify ourselves with our physical body and makes us feel like 'I,' 'me' and 'mine.' In Indian scriptures these faculties of the mind are called, respectively as, 'Manas', 'Buddhi', 'Citta', and 'Ahankara'.

What is mind has been dealt thoroughly in the Indian Scriptures. Who wills; who thinks; who feels; who worries; who enjoys; who imagines; who projects; who rejects; who desires; who decides; who creates; who contemplates; who memorises; who moves faster than light; who knows; who is powerful and who knows he is knowing is called the mind.

Most of the time, our thoughts are spontaneous, unconnected, irrelevant and illogical. Secondly, the mind gets attracted towards negative thoughts easily than towards positive thoughts such as news about violence, disasters, criticism or gossip. We must understand one thing, the thoughts that dominate our mind shapes our external world and also our destiny in it. We attract what we fear, and we get what we expect.

We have learnt partially about the brain and its functions. Let us simplify the definition of mind. Mind (Manas) can be defined as flow of thoughts. Just as we call flowing water as river, not stagnant water. Similarly, a single thought cannot be called mind, but only flow of thoughts.

All learned people have travelled extensively and consolidated their thoughts which we see in many philosophy books. Many enlightened people saw the sufferings of people and became philosophers. They pondered on several issues: self-identity, purpose of life, disease, old age and death. They thought why life is so uncertain, and why people, knowing death is inevitable one day, and they prefer miserable life to death. All these concerns plunged many thinkers into the depths of despair.

However there are few who understood the mind and conquered over all the above concerns and enjoyed mental bliss and liberation. 'If Self or God does not exist what are you going to lose by contemplating on it; If It does exist, you can cross over the ocean of the sorrows by contemplating on it'. This was the motto of Rishis who succeeded in liberating themselves.

Most of us live with contradictions in our mind. Each person has his own views, pre-conceived opinions and beliefs; 'my view', 'your view'. A person expects another person with similar views; if not dis-likeness arises. Generally, I sticks to my view and you stick to your view. This is the root cause for conflicts around the world. Both ignore there is also a 'Correct view' that exists which can be probed. A person's opinions are formed in his mind due to contact with parents, friends or reading books. Sometimes these opinions reflect in his behaviour. He never tries to compare and find whether his views are correct or not. He avoids arguments with parents and friends and continue to live. Even if he finds his view on a particular subject is wrong, he does not readily accepts the new opinion, but sticks to his own. One must remember that if a man continues to live with contradictions in his mind, he can never be happy, though he pretends to be happy. One must be willing to transform himself by acquiring new knowledge. It has been mentioned already; latest brain research confirms that whenever a person learns something new his brain chemistry or neural network is altered permanently.

There are four types of arguments, as presented in Indian scriptures as well as in books on logic: The first one is known as 'Vitanda Vadana' which means a person argues only to suppress the opponent. The second category is known as 'Jalpam', which means a person argues to win over the opponent quoting all sorts of irrelevant statements. In logic, there is one argument: 'the cat has four legs, and the cot also has four legs, therefore, the cot and cat are the same'. It is known such fallacious argument in logic, because of two irrelevant objects are compared. The third type of argument is called 'Vadam' which means argument that arise between two people, who are seriously interested to seek the truth. These types of arguments were being organised by kings and emperors, among scholars, to find the truth, and to reward the winner. The arguments, we see in the court rooms, also fall in this category. The fourth category is known as 'Samvadam', which means the persons questions or argues, with the other, only to know and learn what he doesn't know. The person who questions and argues only to learn new thing which he did not know. He, accepts his ignorance and he wants to be enlightened. This type of questioning and arguments generally happen between a student and teacher. The guru-sishya parampara of ancient Indian education system was following this. In Bhagavad Gita, the question- answer sessions, between Lord Krishna and warrior Arjun, were of this type. Therefore, a 'will' to transform by learning is the prerequisite for obtaining knowledge.

8.2 POWER OF MIND

The mind has tremendous creative power. All technology developments, from bridges to rockets, we see around, stand as a proof of this power of mind. The concepts of space and time are creations of mind. There are many instances where a person, though he is severely injured in a bus or train accident, he rescues number of people, ignoring his injuries. Such feats cannot be explained just by the physical strength of a person. It is due to the power of the mind.

Imagine for a moment the minds of winning athletes, creators and inventors. All have one thing in common: they imagine in their minds that they have expected and achieved their goals, even before the events actually happened. This was revealed by interviews of the winning people. It is widely accepted, to win or succeed in any field, dedication, passion, perfection, faith and will power are needed. These are all created in the minds of positive thinking people.

Another important fact, it seems, is that busy minds cannot create or invent anything in this world. Imagine for a moment, if our ancestors were as busy as we are today, in day to day affairs, they could not have invented anything like motor vehicles, ships or aeroplanes to transport us from one place to another, and also there would have been no great philosophers at all. Therefore, only a free mind can create or invent things.

Your mind can become your friend or your enemy. The concept of friendship or enmity emanates in the mind, and are purely relative and imposed by our minds due to ignorance. When enmity becomes strong it make person resort to crime or cause physical or mental damage to the enemy. When one is in a good mood the entire world looks beautiful. On the other hand, if he is depressed or disgruntled, he may resort to suicide, or involve in anti-social activity.

Similarly, this is my house, this is my wife and this my child all these relationships we form around us. If one critically examines, all these relationships are nothing but creations by the mind. When a child is born, it is the mother which communicates with the child as it grows, and teaches him, saying, this is your father, this is your uncle, etc. Therefore all relations are formed and ingrained in the mind. They are nothing but superimposition by the mind. The concepts of ' I, me and mine' is in the mind and are the root cause of one's selfishness, greed and corruption in the society.

The mind is so fragile it is possible for one to brain wash another person, and make him do whatever he plans to do to the society. This plan can be good for the society, or as we see how terrorists have been brain washed to unleash bombs or commit suicides. This is one form of hypnotising. The followers of a good political or a spiritual leader will do good to the society, while the brain-washed terrorists do great harm to the society.

It is also said, apart from the thought, there is no space or time; all are mental creations.

8.3 THE PERCEPTIVE NATURE OF THE MIND

We are all blessed with five senses and five sense organs; touch, sight, hearing, smell and taste. Without the inner senses the outer sense organs cannot perform their jobs. A man might be having perfect eye balls when seen from outside, but if the image sensing nerves and colour sensing rods and cones are defective, he cannot see objects and their colours. Similarly one might have ear lobes but yet he might be deaf. Each sense operates independently, but it is the mind that integrates the knowledge from different sensory inputs from the sense organs. For example, we touch an object with closed eyes and we can analyse the size of the object, big or small, hot or cold, and soft or hard. Here the signal from the skin of the hand goes to the brain and it is the mind-intellect combination that analyses and decides the nature of the object.

Consider for a while, we are watching a musical concert. Here the retina of the eye receives the light signals from the musician's face, and the ear drum receives the signals from the sounds of the musical instruments and both signals are transmitted simultaneously to the brain, and the mind – intellect analyses and processes the information in an integrated way.

But a question arises who enjoys the concert or when we eat food, who enjoys the taste? To answer these questions, let us consider another example. On a Sunday evening it was raining outside and my programme of visiting someone is dropped. I did not know what to do. I see an advertisement on TV, someone eating a sand witch. Then it strikes my mind, why not I make sandwich. After analysing pros and cons of the desire in the mind, the intellect makes a decision to make a sandwich. Then the intellect makes a planning of how to fulfil the desire, and what are all needed. The mind directs the hands and legs to move and fetch the bread slices, vegetables, sausages, oven etc. When the sandwich is ready I go to the dining table and start eating by activating my teeth, tongue and mouth. But who enjoys the taste. It is not the mouth, not the tongue, not the teeth, and not the brain; the tongue only carries the signal to the brain, and it is my mind that enjoys the taste. The anatomy of karma and mind is presented in the figure (8.3).

If we analyse the whole process, we observe that sitting idle with a void in the mind created the appetite for eating a sandwich. The reason for this void in the mind is due to ignorance. The void is transformed into a proposition and then desire in the mind, and the desire is transformed into action, and finally after eating it is the mind that enjoys the taste. So the starting point for any action is ignorance in the mind, and the ending point also is the mind. So it is the mind that enjoys all our experiences and emotions.

Emotions can be classified as either positive or negative. Positive emotions bring happiness to the mind while negative emotions bring worries to the mind. Emotions such as love and hate; jealous and greed; anger and ego; happiness and sorrow; frustration and revenge are all creations by the mind due to reactions in the mind.

Therefore, the senses operate because of the mind, and the mind needs senses to cognise. When the mind wishes to see, it activates the sense of vision, and when it wants to hear, it activates the ears. When the will of the mind gets reinforced by the desire, it becomes solid like a wall; then whatever the mind desires it experiences it as such. Thus the entire world is anchored in the mind. The disturbances in the mind are due to our actions in the past life and the present life.

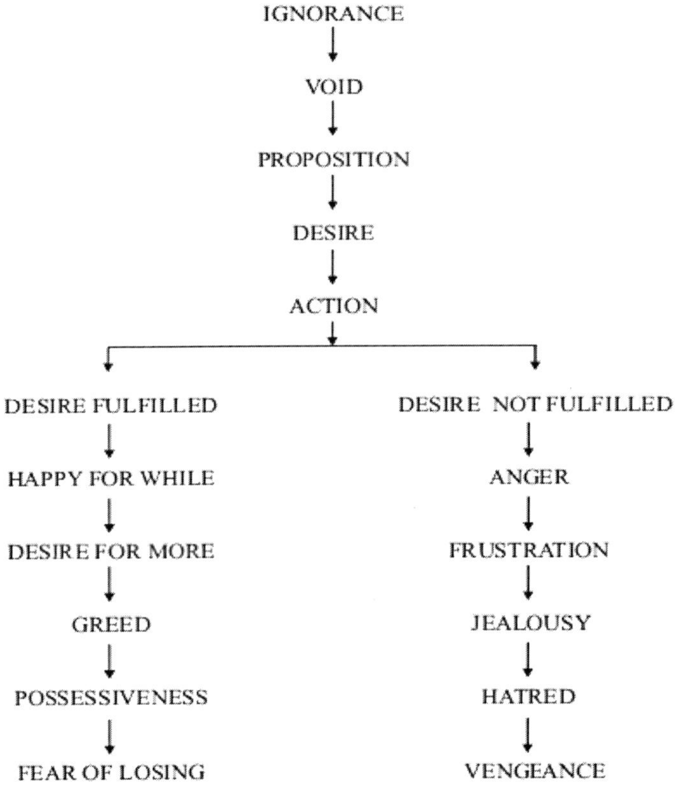

Fig. 8.3 Anatomy of Karma (Action)

As already mentioned, when the mind thinks or desires it is called *mind*; when it makes a decision it is called *intellect;* when it identifies with its physical body, it is called *ego* and when it stores and retracts the stored information, it is known as *memory*. They are respectively called in Indian Scriptures as *Manas*, *Buddh*i, *Ahankara* and *Chitta.* Mind, intellect, ego and memory are different names of the same thing. They are pillars of one formless structure. The mind has the power to will, and it is affected by intellect which decides for us, and it is controlled by our ego, the feeling of *I*, *me* and *mine*. Just like same actor performs different roles in different films, the same mind performs various functions. In this world we derive happiness from two sources: One is from our family members, relatives and friends through exchange of good wishes and pleasantries. The second source of happiness is by possessing materialistic objects from the world. When the desires does not come to us the way we expect, frustration results. Therefore, controlling mind is very important.

8.4 CONTROLLING MIND

We desire for external objects seeking pleasure and happiness in acquiring and possessing them. If the desire is fulfilled, we feel happy. If the desire is not fulfilled, we are frustrated and become angry. If instead of us, someone else possesses the same object we desired, we feel jealousy. Likewise, all emotions and worries arise in the mind. The most important emotions are: happy, unhappy, worry, desire, greed, liking, disliking, hatred, envy, jealousy, anger and revenge.

According to spiritual leader, Sri Sri Ravi Shankar, the worries and feelings cannot function at the same time. That is when we worry we don't feel emotions, and when we are stuck by an emotion worry disappears. Further, it is the mind that worries, and heart that feels. They cannot function at the same time. When your feeling dominates, worry dissolves. Similarly, when you worry a lot your feeling is dead. Feeling when expressed, it drops off. But worry lingers for a longer period of time, and eventually eats you up. Worry always obstructs action. That is when you worry you don't feel like doing any work. But feeling propels action. Therefore, it is necessary to get over the worries. For this again one has to analyse the cause for worry.

All emotions, desires, feelings and worries arise in the mind, and they finally dissolve in the mind. To get over these negative emotions we must understand the working of the mind. It is possible by understanding about the working of the mind, a person can purify or purge his mind of negative thoughts and feelings and be happy.

As mentioned in Bhagavad Gita, for one to have a control over one's mind, he must imagine his consciousness is the *king*, his 'mind is the *'minister'*, his 'Buddhi' is the 'commander', and all the 'sense organs' are the *soldiers.* Generally, the minister takes direct charge and pass on the orders to the commander and soldiers. This should not happen. The mind should not act without the permission of the king. When a person could achieve this, we can say he conquered his mind.

Once you know the cause, you can take a corrective measure. For example when you are watching a movie if you get entangled with the characters on the screen you experience similar emotions as the characters in the film. On the other hand, if you remind yourself that the characters are nothing but the projection and movement of images on a white screen, you won't react to the emotions or feelings as the characters. If one imagines that the whole world is a movie and we are the characters in such a large scale movie, we simply become observers of events and be happy. On the other hand, if we are ignorant, we get entangled in the web. Therefore, if we can train our minds to be a witness to the happenings in the world, we don't get entangled.

Another spiritual leader, Swami Paripoornanda Saraswati, says, that the mind has two sides like that of a coin. The flow of thoughts is the mind, and also the observer of those thoughts is also the same mind. For, example, I imagine a rose flower, immediately the red rose appears in the mind; next imagine an elephant, next a river and next a mountain, the images of these thoughts are projected one after the other in a sequence. Now think, who observed these flow of thoughts that is again me. If you analyse these carefully, we conclude that the formless mind can imagine many forms or any form it wants. Secondly, the thoughts can flow at a speed faster than the sound waves or light waves, and lastly, the mind is the projector as well as the observer.

The great saint Vasishta says "The mind can be controlled in future, but the future is nothing but our hopes and desires which are nothing but the mind; so we fall in the trap. Therefore, how the mind that creates so many unconnected, irrelevant and spontaneous thoughts, can be controlled. The great saint said, it is not necessary to control the mind at all. The mind becomes unruly, only when it is not observed, just like a naughty child does all mischiefs when it is not under watchful eyes. So, to conquer the mind all we have to do is to watch its activities. Mind is the link between the phenomenal world and Supreme Consciousness. Once we transcend mind success follows easily in any field of our pursuit."

A stress in the consciousness reflects as a thought, and continuous stream of thoughts is known as 'mind', according to Saint Ashta Vakra. The illusory world of names and forms is a projection by the mind on the Consciousness. When this illusion-creating and delusion- breeding stresses are removed, thoughts cease, and the mind becomes calm, and hallucination of the world rolls away.

The triple source of sorrow are: Adhi-bhautik, Adhyatmik, and Adhi-daivik. Adhi-bhautik means the source of sorrow lies external to the subject, sentient beings or the insentient objects of the world can cause sorrow. Your enemies or loss of your possessions can cause sorrow.

Adhyatmik source of sorrow lies in the planes of body, mind and intellect. One becomes affected by one disease or the other to make him unhappy. Mind and intellect are also the causes of ignorance as well as knowledge. Most of the suffering is due to ignorance. Only knowledge can remove ignorance.

The last one is Adhi-daivik, which means a man can plunge into sorrow due to nature's fury which is beyond the control of human beings. For example, earth quakes, floods, etc. are considered acts of god.

The end of joy is sorrow, and the end of sorrow is joy. These two are for living beings as inescapable like day and night. Only a man of knowledge can transcend both sorrow and joy.

Taking the objects of the world to be real, the mind goes out entertaining a desire to acquire, to possess and to enjoy. Thus we create a world of struggles riddled with stresses and strains. Once a person realises the external world is just a play comprising of living beings and insentient and inert elements, one transcends all sorrows as the mind becomes quiet.

8.5 THREE CONSCIOUS STATES OF MIND

We have seen the working of the brain and different theories about how consciousness evolves from brain's activity. No single theory is complete. This is understandable as scientists are making serious efforts only recently to understand brain and mind. The scientists at the Howard Hughes Medical Institute, Maryland, found that one adult brain neuron has over thousand gene mutations that alter genetic code. The majority of these mutations are observed when the genes are active and neuron's genome is found to be unique. We do not know when scientists end up the study and come to clear understanding about consciousness. Science is more than four centuries old. Yet we have not fully understood the nature of the subatomic particles. We have discovered more than 200 subatomic particles so far within the atom. Similarly on the cosmology, we were thinking we discovered more. But we discovered only 5% of the universe that is visible, that too, incompletely. Still 95% comprises of unknown dark matter and dark energy yet to be explored.

This way we do not know how much we learnt about the functioning of the brain, may be less than 10%. We just started to learn. We often mistake the instrument for the performer and consider thoughts as product of brain as if they are hormones produced by a gland. Thinking is no more a product of a brain than music is a product of piano. For example, by some arrangement, if you make musician invisible, the ignorant audience think the music is coming from the piano. Understanding consciousness, therefore, is a complex thing. We will see whether consciousness is a product of the brain or vice versa.

Cognition is a kind of relation between the subject's consciousness and the object. How could interaction occur between the inactive self and the active matter which is unconscious? This is the most important epistemological question faced by the cognitive scientists and philosophers alike. The subject knows because of complacence with another object, it knows of its own knowing, and it knows an object in the act of knowing. The theory of knowledge was extensively dealt in the West by scholars like Hume, Cartesian, Kant and Berkeley, while in the East, theory of knowledge was dealt by Sri Ramanuja and Adi Sankara. According to Hume, causality is the link between two events that regularly succeed one another. He questioned Cartesian's belief in the centrality of the mind. Berkeley, in 1929, ultimately denied the existence of the material world, and placed faith in the primacy of the Self.

Cognition, according to the Advaita philosophy, or theory of knowledge by Sankara, is the act of grasping the object by enveloping it with consciousness. His doctrine is that the object's existence depends on it being known. It is interesting to note this theory postulated more than 2000 years ago is very much similar to the modern theories like quantum mechanics which accepts particle-wave dual nature of matter and we observe only one of its nature by the type of experiment the observer chooses to conduct.

Sankara, to prove his theory of knowledge, analyses different conscious states, the human mind experiences during the day and night. Every day one experiences the three states: Waking conscious state (Jagruti), the dream conscious state (Swapna) and deep sleep conscious state(Sushupti).

8.5.1 Waking Conscious State(Jagruti)

In the waking state the sensory organs are active and with the interaction of these senses with the environment, we experience the external world. As explained earlier, it is the mind, through the inner senses, that gathers the information about the objects of the world. We utilise five senses; sight, hearing, smell, taste and touch to gather the information about the object and send it to the brain. However, it is the mind which analyses and decides the nature of the object. Sankara questions the reliability of this knowledge provided by these five senses. We often mistake a mirage for water, a rope for a snake, and an object's appearance changes depending on the angle from which we are looking at. A spoon dipped in water appears bent. Therefore the big question is, how to judge what we see in the waking state is real or unreal.

One must define what reality is? It has been defined in the scriptures, Reality as one that does not undergo any change, which does not take birth, which cannot be divided into parts and which is eternal. Only one eternal thing can exist in this universe. If a second reality exists, it forfeits the definition. The reality can be established, according Sankara and scriptures, only by the process of elimination of doubts.

The external world or universe comprises of only three things: Space, Time, and Matter. According to Einstein's theory of relativity, space, time and matter can expand or contract depending on the speed at which they move. They also undergo change depending on the gravitational field. Moreover space and time are integral part constituting, what is known as, one space-time continuum. Time is a creation of mind, space-time continuum is nothing but a geometry and is also a creation of mind, since geometry is a creation of the mind. Matter can exist as a particle or wave depending on the observer's mind. We have already learnt why and how the world is not real. Adi Sankara, some 2000 years back analysed the unreality through his interpretation of the Mandukya Upanishad. Since the phenomenal world of duality is a creation of ignorance, it can be eradicated only with right kind of knowledge.

Sankara, in support of his theory, that waking state is not real, quotes that the illusions like mirage and mistaking rope for a snake. These illusions cannot come into existence without a substratum. Entities exist in their own substratum on which they are superimposed. A rope appears as a snake because it has some qualities of snake at its substratum. When a light shines on the rope, the elimination of snake from the rope occurs simultaneously with the knowledge of discrimination between the rope and the snake. The snake is superimposed on the rope. All entities, produced as a reflection of reality (Consciousness), are true as long as their substratum is kept in view.

The Schrodinger's dead-alive cat paradox is well known. This led John Wheeler saying the whole universe may owe its real existence to the fact that it is being observed. In other words, the mind is the creator of the universe.

Sankara quotes another example. A stick immersed in a glass of water appears bent. This, according to Sankara, is due to illusion. However, according to science, we know it is due to refraction of light. When we immerse our hand in water we come to know it is not bent. But Sankara says after knowledge dawns, the illusion must disappear, but it is not happening. Therefore the knowledge of science is incomplete and hence, some other knowledge is needed to eliminate it. That other knowledge will again require a third knowledge for a similar purpose and so on. Therefore, to avoid this contingency, the final knowledge must be self-immolating.

We all know how small we were when we were in mother's womb as a seed, without any development of organs like hands, feet and eyes. We acquire some shape after fifth month or so. We existed without a proper form or name. We are given a name by parents only few days after birth. At birth, our legs, hands, chest, and face were small. As we grew the body also grew. The question is, how we know that we have grown from a small child to a six feet tall human being. Unless there is someone or something within us that has not undergone any change we wouldn't be able to notice we have grown. This is known as the individual "self." This self is not inside any part of my physical body. This self is the observer of all changes taking place in the world as well, and the images or thoughts that sweep the mind.

Nothing is static in this universe. The earth is rotating about it's own axis at a speed of 0.5 km per second, and at the same time it is also the sun at a speed of 30 km per second, and the solar system is going round the centre of our galaxy at a speed of about 600 km per second. Unless there is some fixed reference we cannot judge the ever changing world. Also, the universe or the world we see is not there in the beginning, and it will vanish at some point in future. If we do not accept the Sankara's unreality principle we end up concluding all illusory world as real.

"A thing that does not exist in the beginning and do not exist at the end, cannot exist in the middle." This statement from the Mandukya Upanishad, which can be called the law of unreality,

was often quoted by Sankara in support of his illusory world. Anything which has name and form must have been created at one time or other. Anything that has been created, will necessarily vanish or disappears one day. Everything, we see around in this world, has name and form since they have been created. They did not exist in the beginning, and do not exist at the end. During the transitory state as we see them, must be illusory in nature, and cannot be real.

Matter is made up of atoms, and atom comprises of a nucleus containing neutrons and protons while electrons revolve around this nucleus. Scientists proved that these subatomic particles exhibit dual nature. That is they are neither particles nor waves. They are both. Their appearance depends on the experiment the observer chooses to conduct. The double-slit experiment amply proved this. The question is, if the subatomic particles constituting the atom are not real how the matter comprising of atoms can be taken to be real?

Quantum physicists discovered that physical atoms are made up of vortices of energy that are constantly spinning and vibrating, each one radiating its own unique energy signature. Therefore, if we really want to observe ourselves and find out what we are, we are really beings of energy and vibration, radiating our own unique energy signature -this is the fact what quantum physics has shown us time and again. We are much more than what we perceive ourselves to be, and it's time we begin to see ourselves in that light. If we observed the composition of an atom with a microscope, you would see a small, invisible tornado like vortex, with a number of infinitely small energy vortices called quarks and photons. These are what make up the structure of the atom. As you focused in closer and closer on the structure of the atom, you would see nothing; you would observe a physical void. The atom has no physical structure or boundary. We too have no physical structure, and physical things really don't have any physical structure! Atoms are made out of invisible energy, not tangible matter. All material objects in the world are made up of atoms, if an atom has no structure, how can the world, we see, be real?

This illusory appearance has been identified by Sankara as due to Maya. Sankara, therefore, concludes that the phenomenal world as it appears in the waking state is nothing but the projection of Reality. The worldly objects which has only names and forms as support for their existence, are in fact due to our false perception. A pot made out of clay has no existence apart from clay. The pot has a name and form. Before the pot is made there was only clay. When the pot is destroyed it will become only clay. In this context, the clay is real and pot is unreal. Similarly we can say about the ocean and its waves. The wave is also water and ocean is also water. So wave has no existence in reality. Similarly a ring made of gold has no existence, it is only gold in reality. Ring has no value, but only gold has.

Our thoughts connect us to the external world. This is my house, this is my wife, this is my child, this is my uncle, this is my neighbour. Our thoughts revolve around these repeatedly and we are caught in the web. Close your eyes for few seconds and empty the mind of these thoughts, the outside world does not exist. For example, there is a vacant site or land measuring 40' x 60 ft. The person starts constructing a house and in the process he builds walls to separate the bed room from the dining room, etc. Before the walls rise, the space is one, but once the walls are built it creates separation of space since it gets divided..

When we close our eyes and imagines different objects, they appear one after the other; unconnected and irrelevant, these thoughts come in succession as if in a dream. This is the power of mind that can project, accept or reject objects of thoughts. Finally when we have to sleep we have to say, 'my dear mind, please windup all your thoughts, I want to sleep'.

8.5.2 Dream State Consciousness (Swapna)

Dreams are appearance of images, ideas, emotions, and sensations that occur in succession. They are, usually, appear in the mind, involuntarily, during certain part of our sleep. The content and purpose of dreams are not definitely understood, though they have been a topic of scientific speculation, as well as a subject of philosophical and religious interest, throughout recorded history. The scientific study of dreams is called 'oneirology.' Dreams mainly occur during the Rapid Eye Movent stage of sleep,—when brain activity is high and resembles that of being awake. REM sleep is revealed by continuous movements of the eyes during sleep. At times, dreams may occur during other stages of sleep. However, these dreams tend to be much less vivid or memorable.

The length of a dream can vary; they may last for a few seconds, or approximately 20–30 minutes. People are more likely to remember the dream if they are awakened during the REM phase. The average person has three to five dreams per night, and some may have up to seven; however, most dreams are immediately or quickly forgotten. Dreams tend to last longer as the night progresses. During a full eight-hour night sleep, most dreams occur in the typical two hours of REM.

In modern times, dreams have been seen as a connection to the unconscious mind. They range from normal and ordinary to overly surreal and bizarre. Dreams can be of varying natures, such as being frightening, exciting, magical, melancholic, adventurous, or sexual. The events in dreams are generally outside the control of the dreamer, with the exception of lucid dreaming, where the dreamer is self-aware. Dreams can at times make a creative thought occur to the person or give a sense of inspiration. Poets, inventors, creative writers, philosophers have had such mystic inspirations as reported in various books. Even Einstein is supposed to have formulated his revolutionary theories in sub-conscious or dream state.

When we close our eyes and drift off to sleep, something in our mind spins up fanciful tales of teeth falling out, bouncing around in giant marshmallows in the sky, taking a walk in the park, or going in a rocket or a spaceship. Common as they are, there's not a lot of definitive science on how we dream. Are dreams the work of the imagination, or the work of some reflex in the brain? A team of French researchers suggest at its most basic, dreaming is generated by the brainstem, the part of the brain that connects to the spinal cord and plays a role in regulating sleep, a "bottom-up" process rather than a result of the brain's higher functions. The study looked at patients with auto-activation deficit, a syndrome characterized by extreme apathy. People with such a deficit lose the ability to spontaneously activate any cognitive or emotional processes. They report that they don't have any thoughts at all, called "mental emptiness." They often sit quietly in the same place all day without speaking or moving. If someone prompts them, they can answer questions and recall memories, but left to their own, their minds remain blank. So if these patients don't have spontaneous thoughts, do they dream?

About 13 auto-activation deficit subjects and 13 healthy control subjects were asked to keep a dream diary, which the researchers then analysed for length, complexity and bizarreness. Not all the auto-activation deficit patients reported dreaming, but some did. Those who reported dreaming (only four out of the 13) had shorter, less bizarre dreams than the control groups; dream about normal scenarios like walking or shaving, according to the LA Times. Not sitting in a park and watching a dog turning into a wolf.

The patients who don't have spontaneous thoughts during the day can do so when asleep, suggests that dreaming might be a bottom-down process, essentially a reflex. But the simplicity and lack of emotional resonance of their dreams suggest that higher-order processes are required to create the strange scenarios most people find in their dreams. The full study was published in *Brain* journal.

Now let us look what is presented in Mandukya Upanishad about the dream conscious state as understood by Sankara.

In a dream, we experience objects and events which are unconnected and illogical. We declare the falsity of objects in a dream, because of location of the objects inside the body and because of their contraction in size. Objects as small as a needle and as big as an elephant or a mountain are perceived inside the mind in a contracted form.

One may dream of visiting a foreign country, and we feel it is false taking into account the distance and time involved in travelling. However, the experiences of dream state and waking state are not very much different because we dream what we experience in waking state like going places, conversing with people, exchanging feelings of love and sorrow. Dreams, even though have some novel features like flying in the air, they are held as mere appearances due to the imagination by a dreamer. A man in the waking state also can dream similar things as is called day-dreaming. Dream objects, like objects in waking state are conditioned by cause and effect. Both states are not real, being caused by false perception and imagination.

An objection to this concept of unreality by Sankara been raised often on the following ground. The objects of waking state, say, food, drink, a car are seen to fulfil some purpose like satisfying hunger, thirst and transportation, but objects of dream state serve no such purpose. This refutation has been clarified by Sankara. For a man, who has got his hunger appeased and thirst quenched by eating and drinking in the waking state, as soon as he sleeps, he dreams as though afflicted by thirst and hunger as if he was fasting the whole day. This is similar to the case, after getting full satisfaction in the dream from eating and drinking, he wakes up to feel hunger and thirst. Thus the objects of waking state are contradicted in dream and object of dream are contradicted in waking state. Therefore, both states, being originated from imagination are equally unreal.

The fact that objects perceived by the mind in dream are mere mental impressions having an obscurity, while objects experienced by the same mind during waking state, like seeing an object and hearing a music have vividness. This is not due to the existence of objects themselves, since their distinction is noticed even in dream, but caused by differences in organs of perception. Hence it is stated that the objects of the waking state are as much creation of imagination as the dream objects.

An individual is possessed a kind of memory. From the apprehension of some fancy as the cause, follows the apprehension of the result. From this causal relation, there arises the memory of the cause and effect, from which follows their apprehension as well as awareness of action. This apprehension of causality, leads to the awareness of different results following from those actions. From the awareness of objects, arises memory and from this memory again arises their awareness. In this way an individual imagines diverse things, both personal and external that are mutually the cause and effect.

The unreality of waking and dream states was expressed by a Chinese philosopher in a simple statement: "last night I dreamt I was a butterfly. Now I don't know I am a man who dreamt he was a butterfly or a butterfly who dreamt now it is a man."

8.5.3 Deep Sleep State of Consciousness (Sushupti)

During deep-sleep state, all energy goes into recharging your batteries: Your kidneys clean your blood, your organs detoxicate, cells are replaced, wounds heal, and muscle tissue builds up. Moreover, you consolidate your memories. If one gets too little deep sleep, his immune system becomes weak. Over the long period, if one is deprived of deep sleep, he might suffer fatigue, apathy and even depression. How much deep sleep a person must get? *A healthy dose of deep sleep needed for an average man is about 20% of overall sleep duration.* This is so assuming there are three phase of sleep. But there's a fourth phase and this is where things get interesting:

The Mandukya Upanishad dealt with the deep-sleep state in a different way as explained by Sankaracharya. An individual, in deep sleep, neither desires any enjoyable things nor see any dream. He becomes a mass of mere consciousness and everything becomes undifferentiated. In deep sleep one enjoys great happiness, but this not bliss.

When our body goes to deep sleep 42 parts of our body take rest, just like all birds settle down on a tree at sunset. These are: Organs of action-5; sense organs-5; gross elements-5; objects of organs of action-5; objects of senses-5; subtle body (mind, intellect, ego and memory)-4; objects of contemplation of the subtle body-4; taijasa-1; prana-1; dharana-1; and prajna-1; When we wake in the morning, these parts again wake up and start their functions. The Gross body comprising of skin, flesh, bones, etc. is totally inactive like a log of wood during deep-sleep state. The subtle body, comprising of mind, intellect, ego and memory is totally absent. Only breathing and heart beat will continue.

An individual gets up in the morning, and says he had nice sleep last night. Since mind is absent during deep sleep, it can be said that mind is not the self who experienced the happiness, during deep sleep, is the individual 'I' or 'Self,' and not the mind. This happiness, one enjoys during deep sleep is same for a wealthy man who sleeps in an air conditioned room, or a beggar who sleeps on the footpath. As the vibrations of the mind, in deep sleep, is absent one is said to be free from any effort and is said to be happy.

In waking state, one experiences the gross objects of the external world, and in dream he experiences the objects internally. But in deep sleep, he becomes a mass of consciousness that keeps on oscillating between the waking state and dream state. Thus deep-sleep state becomes a doorway to the other two states of consciousness. According to the Upanishads, the eye is the place of experiencing the objects in the waking state, mind is the place of experiencing objects during dream, and space within the heart is the place of experiencing deep-sleep state.

Deep-sleep, by virtue of it being a state of sleep, is conditioned by cause alone, whereas waking- state and dream state are conditioned by cause and effect. Dream has been described as false perception, and deep-sleep has been mentioned of as darkness consisting of non-perception of reality. Waking and dream states are endued with dream and sleep and for that reason they are conditioned by cause and effect. Non-perception of reality is common to all the three states, but deep-sleep is distinguished by absence of desire. This absence of desire is the main cause of happiness in deep sleep. The person in deep sleep is said to be undifferentiated; since whole host of duality he experiences in the waking and dream states, which are due to modifications of the mind, becomes non-discernible in deep sleep state, just as the day and its phenomenal world becomes non-discernible under the cover of darkness in the night. Conscious experiences which are nothing but vibrations of the mind in the waking and dream states, become solidified during deep-sleep state.

After a good deep sleep, how a person gets up in the morning? The last thought that comes to the mind, before a person goes to sleep is responsible for waking him up. Sometimes it is more accurate than an alarm clock. Suppose a person has to catch an early morning flight, and he wants to get up by 4:30 in the morning. Once he sets up this in his mind before going to sleep, even by chance the alarm does not ring, since he might have set as PM instead of AM, but still he gets up. Here the individual self "I" gets up first, and wakes up the mind first, after some transition, the mind wakes up the intellect and the senses, and lastly the gross body is activated, and the physical activity starts for the day. The 'I' feeling spreads out through out the body, just like waves spread out when a stone is dropped in a still water in a pond.

In Upanishad, the waking-state consciousness is called "Visva," the dream state consciousness is known as "Taijasa" and deep-sleep conscious state is called "Prajna." Though deep sleep has been described, sometimes, as *bliss*, it is conditioned by causal state *darkness* and is born of seed of ignorance. In deep sleep one comprehends neither Truth not falsehood. In deep-sleep the knower and the known is merged into one and so he enjoys happiness. Therefore deep-sleep is conditioned by non-perception of Reality which is the seed of false perception.

Dream belongs to one who sees falsely and sleep belongs to one who does not know the Reality. When the individual, sleeping under the influence of errors and ignorance, is awakened by the right knowledge, he realises the birthless, dreamless, sleepless, non-duality that is *Real.* This is Truth and its realisation comes from Knowledge only.

9 TRUE KNOWLEDGE

9.1 TRUE AND FALSE

Lies can be many, but truth will be one. When a thief is caught by the police he keeps on telling different lies and stories during interrogation. Finally he breaks down and tells the truth. The interrogation ends once the truth is known. This is same in every field of knowledge.

In our daily life, whenever we read the news or hear from a colleague, we feel a natural instinct to find the truth in what we hear or read. Often we cross check the source of information for its authenticity. In other words, we attempt to infer truth from what we perceive.

A judge in a court, for example, tries to extract truth from the arguments from the plaintiff's side as well as defence side. However, all judgments may not turn out to be true for a number of reasons. Firstly, the judge concerned must be a perfect subject without any mental or sensual defects. Secondly, the witnesses must be honest and lastly, the arguments by the lawyers must be complete. These conditions are not satisfied always, and that is why, probably, we have lower courts and higher courts for justice. Therefore, a judgement arrived purely by logical grounds may not necessarily represent the truth.

Scientists, all over the world, are working towards Grand Unification Theory that would explain all forces of nature.

That is, a single physical law would be adequate to explain all phenomena, right from the subatomic processes up to the origin of the universe. Once this single law is found, many scientists believe, what it attains is not another approximation to the endless road to the truth, but Truth itself. Moving towards this goal, scientists are inventing new theories, abandoning the old theories. Super symmetry and Super gravity theories are few among them. Obviously, if there is to be a total unification of physical laws, it has to lead up to very complex degree of symmetry. Further, if we are also made up of the same atoms and molecules, these symmetries must be such as to include human consciousness also. Scientists are far away from this goal, and the reasons are plenty.

Science knowledge is perceptive knowledge. It is obtained from the five senses and processed by the brain. It involves knowledge about the world we perceive. It has been already mentioned that senses always do not provide correct information, sometimes it can be illusory. It is not reliable since perceptive knowledge depends on many factors.

Imperfections in science knowledge can be explained through our everyday experiences. For example, when we see an object that appears as red in colour, from the first principles of interactions of light and matter, we conclude that the redness of the object is due to the material property of the object, by which the object absorbs all the six colours of the white light except red colour it reflects. That is the surface of the object reflects only red photons. However, if we shine a monochromatic light of different wavelength, we see the same object in a different colour instead of red. This proves redness is not the property of the object but of light falling on it. Since sun is the source of light, we can say the sun is responsible for the colourful world we see. But even this does not seem to be right knowledge because unless we are blessed with the organ eye, with cones and rods, we cannot perceive different colours.

For example, a colour blind man sees an object in a different colour than a normal man.

Scientists thus attribute colour of an object to the wavelength of light emitted by it. However, when we energize an atom, neither the electron that is excited nor the photon that is emitted has any property called "colour."

We are yet to understand the complete mechanism of type and form of information and how it is processed by the brain or mind. For this, theories after theories have to be postulated. Even then to understand finally who enjoys the function of seeing, hearing, tasting, touching or smelling, which can be pleasant or unpleasant, a new type of knowledge is needed.

Therefore, knowledge, in order to be true, should be definite, so that it does not leave one in doubt and must be unambiguous and clear. So True knowledge can be defined as "the process of cognition which reveals or establishes the true nature of the subject, and the object, and the relation between them." This can be put it in another form, saying, 'knower', 'known' and the process of 'knowing' must be made clear by the knowledge. The Self-knowledge is a state where the' knower', the' known' and the 'act of knowing' merges into one.

As far as the subject is concerned it is difficult to establish its true nature unless we are able answer the question- "Who am I?" Similarly on the object side, we are not pretty sure whether the knowledge provided by the senses is reliable or not, taking into account the particle-wave dual nature of matter, and illusions caused by the environment. Unless we know the origin of the object, namely, how it came into existence, and its atomic and subatomic nature, we cannot find the true nature of the object. Unless we know the true natures of the subject and the object we cannot establish their relation.

The main difference between a scientist and a spiritualist is this: While the scientist does research on the external objects he perceives, the spiritualists have done research on themselves. That is, spiritualist will try to know the knower, which is known as meta-cognition. This takes us to the fundamental question –mind or matter, which came first?

9.2 INTUITIVE KNOWLEDGE

Intuitive knowledge is another form of knowledge which does not depend on the five senses. According to epistemology of eastern thinkers, knowledge can be obtained through five different means: Direct cognition, indirect knowledge, knowledge by comparison, knowledge by negation and finally knowledge by verbal testimony. Intuitive knowledge falls in the category of direct knowledge. It is called by different names. The person seeking knowledge contemplates on it in a subconscious or super conscious state and receives a revelation. It is said the origin of scriptures like "Vedas," "Bible" and "Quran" are the result of revelations by great people. So the intuitive knowledge is revealed during the homogeneous conscious state of the contemplator is without error, without discrimination or comparison. However the degree of truthfulness of such revelations depends on the conscious state of the person at that particular point of time, since the scriptures are the result of series of such revelations.

When Einstein published his General Theory of Relativity, it was considered a great leap, decades ahead of contemporary physicists. It took hundred years to prove his theories are true to science. According to this theory, the size of the object and its mass depends on its speed. How could he formulate such revolutionary theories? The theory that reveals equivalence principle between matter and energy is another case in point. Such knowledge is possible only through intuition. Intuition takes birth as a result of enquiry supported by deep contemplation.

Direct knowledge through intuition by a perfect subject will have universal significance. Eternal knowledge or laws can be formulated only through intuition, and not by perceptive knowledge. Therefore, intuitive knowledge is due to super sensory perception that involves no mediation or inference. It is transcendental, unlimited in range and intensity due to purity of mind. The highest knowledge is attained neither by perception through the senses which are particulars, nor by inferences which present generalities, but only by super-sensory perception or intuition. For more clarity, we may say the external world is perceived while the internal or spiritual is intuited. Intuition is a fundamental type of cognition capable of comprehending the true and true only, when the subject is freed from all defects, and possesses untainted mind and sharp intellect.

For example, the origin of Vedas cannot be traced to a single person or period. They are the result of many Rishis who meditated and contemplated to find the truth behind human existence, purpose and goal of life. They considered human body as a laboratory, and researched for Truth behind creation of the Universe and the human mind. Scientists, like Einstein, also followed the same route to hypothesise a law or theory for a particular phenomenon in the realm of materialistic world, whereas the Rishis meditated on the reality behind the existence of life and the universe. Secondly, the level of contemplation and meditation to find the truth behind God and Nature were entirely at a different conscious level. So, the Vedas, are the result of cumulative search, in a systematic way, and the Vedas are the result of integration of all the outcomes by different Rishis at different time periods. These were passed on from person to person verbally until they could be put into writing. They invented a method of memorising so that the content is not corrupted over a period of time.

There are six orthodox schools of Indian philosophies: Nyaya, Vaiseshika, Samkhya, Yoga, Purva Mimamsa and Uttara Mimamsa. Of these six schools, only the last two are connected with the Vedas. These last two are not mentioned in the Buddhistic literature.

The Vedas were compiled by sage Veda Vyasa, who divided them into four parts entrusting the work two four Rishis: Rigveda comprising of 21 sections were written by Rishi by name Pyla; the Yajurveda comprising of 109 sections was compiled by Rishi by name Vyshampayana; the Sama Veda with 1000 sections was compiled by Rishi by name Jaimuni, and Athervana Veda comprising of 50 sections was compiled by Rishi by name Sunandana.

These four Vedas can be broadly divided into ritual texts, and knowledge texts. Broadly speaking they are aimed at providing the means as how to conduct oneself in this world, or lead a life, so that it enables him to achieve the final goal of his existence.

The Upanishads were the result of integration of all knowledge texts of the Vedas. Since Upanishads did not contain any ready-made consistent system of thought, there arose the necessity of 'Brahma Sutras' by Badarayana and Vyasa. So, Brahma Sutra contained systematized philosophy of the Upanishads. Adi Sankaracharya discovered the highest Truth by churning, Bhagavad Gita, Upanishads, and Brahma Sutras, and he has written commentaries on them.

The knowledge contained in the above three scriptures, speak only the voice of intuition, where one can search and discover Truth. According to Sankara, the proponent of monistic philosophy, known as Advaita, the knowledge arising out of the integration of knowledge texts of the Vedas, Upanishads and Bhagavat Gita constitute the Highest Knowledge that is Birth less. This Highest knowledge is one, knowing which, the seeker feels nothing else need to be known. For this reason it is called Birthless or Eternal knowledge.

Many of us live in this world with lot of contradictions in our mind and not cable of distinguishing what is right and what is wrong. My friend is right or I am right. Finally, we compromise with different views on a particular subject, and continue to live with duality or multiple views. As it is said, we always come across three views: 'My view', 'your view' and the 'correct or right view'. Generally each one sticks to his own view and never make a serious attempt to arrive at the correct view. This is considered, unfortunately a system of respecting other's view. Such people will not have the intellectual ability to learn the Highest Truth.

Interestingly, multiple views are not allowed in the sphere science. If two scientists present two different theories about a single physical phenomenon, both will be suspected of errors and ignorance, or at the most one theory is accepted, but never both the theories can be correct at the same time about one and same phenomenon. Same logic is followed in search of spiritual Truth. Therefore, the Highest Knowledge alone can remove the ignorance from the mind of the seeker. If ignorance persists even after attaining knowledge, then that knowledge cannot be called as birth-less or true, because we need another kind of knowledge to remove the ignorance. If ignorance persists still, we may require third or fourth knowledge. To avoid such a contingency, the "Birthless" knowledge has been defined as self-immolating, merging cause and effect. So, the Highest Truth can be discovered only through Birth-less knowledge. This knowledge is eternal.

The brains filing system is same for all of us. Whenever we learn something new the brain circuit changes permanently in a systematic way. This is the latest discovery in brain-science. Our bodies are shaped by genes, our genes are shaped by our brains, and our brains are shaped by our knowledge, Therefore, when we learn new knowledge as how to be happy in all circumstances, that knowledge will remain permanently in our brain circuit. Therefore, such a knowledge becomes highest knowledge that is eternal.

When an enlightened person has to explain the Pure Conscious State or Bliss, which he discovered and experienced, to another person, it will be very difficult. This state has no name or form and hence it is unexplainable. To explain such a knowledge to a disciple, the guru follows a systematic way of negations to transmit the highest knowledge, by saying, not this, not this, until all possible perceptions and conclusions are excluded.

9.3 PURE CONSCIOUSNESS (TURIYA)

Suppose, we take a man, blind folded, in a rocket to the moon, without his knowledge, and unfold him. The conscious experience for the first few moments can be imagined as pure consciousness. For few moments, the mind is not operational, the person does not know where he is, and what is around. After few moments, his mind starts extracting previously stored information, and start comparing to decide where he is currently.

Everyone, after his daily routine, goes to sleep in the night. During the day he sees and interacts with people and objects. When he goes to sleep, he experiences dream state and finally goes into deep sleep. Then he wakes up and the cycle of waking, dream and deep sleep states are repeated. Sleep appears to be providing a gap in the three conscious states, one experiences. However close analysis will prove that there is no gap in the conscious states. For example, a person was reading a novel in the night before sleeping and read up to 25 pages and closes the book and goes to sleep. Next day after waking up he continues reading the book from page 26. If there is a gap in the conscious states this could not have been possible; since mind, intellect, memory and ego are all absent during deep sleep. Therefore, the substratum of all the three conscious states is the witness to all our experiences during waking, dream and deep-sleep states. This Pure Consciousness is a continuous stream without any break. According to

Upanishads, this consciousness continues even after death. So the Consciousness is eternal and is not connected to birth or death of an individual.

It has been proved that all objects of waking state and dream state are not real. This raises a question; who apprehends these objects, and who indeed is their creator? Here, the answer is the Self." The Self-effulgent self, imagines itself through itself cognises the diverse objects.

All such concepts: I am happy, miserable, ignorant, young, old, and diseased, I am enjoyer, I am this, these are all mine, etc. These are all superimposition by the mind on the Self or Consciousness. This self is present in all illusory appearances, and is responsible for all the above mentioned ideas.

If Self is everything; a question naturally arises: there are as many selves as there are individual living beings. This defies the fact that Truth or Reality is one, and cannot be multiple. Truth is only one Supreme Consciousness that pervades and envelopes everything we see and we do not see. Except this Consciousness, nothing exists. We are all participants in an virtual-reality like world. The so called individual self is only the reflection of the Supreme Consciousness. When this Consciousness is reflected in the body, the physical body is activated or illumined; when this Consciousness is reflected in the subtle body, the senses, mind and intellect are illumined, and when it is reflected in the causal body the ignorance is illumined and eliminated.

The cause for illusory world has been described as "Maya" in Upanishads. The cause for Maya, according to Sankara, is the mind that vibrates or oscillates creating the illusions, delusions and hallucinations. As in dream, the mind vibrates as though having dual aspects; so in the waking state, the mind vibrates as though with two facets; the cognisor and the thing cognised. All things that move or do not move are only perceived by the vibrating mind. The oscillating mind causes the three conscious states namely, waking, dream and deep sleep come into existence. When the mind ceases to oscillate, everything merges into the *Self.*

Pure Consciousness has no contact with the objects at any time. An object has no existence, as already deduced, and an illusory object is not different from the awareness. An act of knowing implies an object to be known, but Consciousness that is like the shining of the sun, needs no objects. Besides the sun and shining is the same, though in common parlance a distinction is made. The sun is reflected in the water of a holy river as well as in a dirty pond in the street. The sun shine is not effected in either case. In the same way the Consciousness is not affected by the material world of objects which appear real. This explains that the Consciousness and the world must be one and the same. The Knower, the Known and the Knowledge merge into one Supreme Consciousness.

As long as there is mental preoccupation with causality, so long the worldly states continue. When the engrossment with causality is exhausted, one does not take part in the worldly state with any interest. The subject and the object become mutually the objects of perception to each other. No individual being whatsoever takes birth, it has no source of birth. This non-duality is the highest Truth where nothing whatsoever takes birth.

"Just as in a dream, the human beings rise, fight for their competitive existence, play their sensual games and in the end die away, only to be born again, just like another wave in the ocean. When the mind is at rest, the world of all names and forms must necessarily disappear into Pure Consciousness." This has been stated in Ashta Vakra Gita by Swami Chinmayananda.

"The seat of Pure Consciousness is the substratum for all the imaginary world of body, mind and intellect and their experiences."

10

PATH TO SELF-KNOWLEDGE

10.1 GOOD HEALTH

The person who is seriously interested in spiritual progress, must keep up a good physical health. Good physical health can be achieved by adhering to disciplined life style. It is not only eating a balanced food and exercising or walking, one must know how to eat food, how to breathe, etc. It must be remembered that practice of Yoga improves physical health, while meditation and Pranayama improves mental health.

There are nine openings in our physical body. One must keep them clean and hygienic. One has to take bath twice daily with water neither too hot nor too cold, but just warm water. While taking bath most of us ignore cleaning the naval, where it was found as many as 1400 bacteria survive. Similarly, under the feet and between fingers and arm pits.

Breathing is very important in keeping good health. There are basically two types: diaphragm breathing and the chest expanding type. It is the first one should practice. It is known breathing is connected with body, heart and mind. We experience daily about 73000 thoughts. It is necessary to reduce the number of thoughts to minimum. This can be done by practicing concentration on a single object for a long time, and by practicing breathe regulation exercise known as 'Pranayama' which regulates thoughts and energy flow. One has to lower his breathing rate to achieve good health. It is known animals like tortoise, which breathe only 4 times per minute live 150 years compared human beings who breathe 15 times per minute and live for 70 years on an average.

We have to eat clean food, drink clean water and breathe clean air. Next, what to eat and how to eat significantly affect our health. First it is advisable for spiritual seeker to adopt to vegetarian food which is easily digestible. The stomach volume must be divided into three parts. One part must be filled with solid food, the second part must be filled with liquid food, and the last part must be left vacant to allow for the gases formed during the digestive process. The food we gulp must be bitten or chewed 12 times before it is swallowed. Before eating food, one must recollect where from it came, and thank god for providing it. We can survive only few days without food, few hours without water and few minutes without air.

Every day, the seeker must pray and express gratitude to the parents, sun, earth and his teachers. Without them we do not exist on this planet. Expressing gratitude distinguishes us from animals.

10.2 SELF-DISCIPLINE

The person, seeking Knowledge about his true nature that leads to Bliss in the current life and liberation after death, must cultivate certain discipline in order to become eligible to receive this knowledge. Milk is a food and gives us energy, but to boil milk, the vessel must be cleaned properly so that the milk is not spoiled. To receive the highest knowledge, the mind of the student must be pure and his intellect must be sharp.

To put it in another way, if a person is interested in getting Ph.D. in a particular subject, he has to pass number of qualifying examinations like School Certificate, undergraduate and post graduate exams with distinction. In a similar way, the person seeking the highest knowledge must qualify himself, passing certain exams or criteria. These are six in number as listed in the scriptures:

1. 'Sama' which means Control of sense organs.
2. 'Dama' which means control of external organs.
3. 'Uparati' which means wisdom.
4. 'Titiksha' which means patience.
5. 'Shraddha' which means faith in Guru and the scriptures.
6. 'Mumukshatva' which means determination to achieve Bliss and Moksha.

Control of Internal Organs (Sama) involves restricting the use of the mind (Manas), intellect (Buddhi), memory (Citta) and Ego (Ahankara) and keep them under check. The mind always wanders, desiring this and that. Scientists have recorded that on an average about 73000 thoughts invade one's brain every day. These thoughts most of the times are irrelevant, unconnected, illogical and spontaneous. The mind does not distinguish right from wrong thoughts, useful or useless thoughts. Therefore mind has to be disciplined and its wandering must be restricted. Meditation, and pranayama are prescribed to control thoughts in our mind.

It is intellect that warns the mind don't do this, don't do that which are bad. Often the intellect is over ruled by the mind, that is how we indulge in bad habits knowingly. The intellect must be sharp and clear to down play the mind. Only the intellect has the ability to distinguish right from the wrong.

It is habitual for memory to constantly dig out the past, and highlight only those memories that hurt us. One has to cultivate the habit of forgive and forget attitude. If someone is not happy with you and goes on talking bad about you, just forget and forgive him. You leave him, let him enjoy the happiness he derives by insulting or bad propaganda against you.

The 'Ego' is another which keeps on projecting about oneself. I only did this; I only know this, etc. You should not boast about yourself, it is others who must recognise your effort and appreciate you. We express our attitude or feeling, 'I, me, and mine' in our day to day dealings with people and possessions; one must understand that the 'Ego' is at play behind this attitude. Just imagine the size of the universe, and in that how small a human being is, once you keep this in mind there will not be scope for ego.

These four internal faculties we use to gain knowledge must be purified, properly trained and tuned to know the Ultimate Reality. Prayer, concentration and meditation, and breathe control have been prescribed for achieving this.

Control of External Organs (Dama) is about controlling the five organs we use to interact with the external world. We use our eyes, ears, tongue, nose and skin, hands and legs to do our day to day activity. One must have control over the use of these organs. One must be able to draw a line to what extent we can use them and how we use them and when to retrieve them. The main goal must be in mind, and continually checking whether the activities being performed are, contributing towards the goal or not. We must speak what is in our mind, and we must act according to what we speak.

Wisdom (Uparati) is required in every activity of ours. The world around us comprises of good and bad; virtue and evil, we come across in all facets of life. We need wisdom to manoeuvre ourselves in this world. There is library, and there is bar next to it; there is junk food restaurant and home food; nice book to read, and a horror movie to watch. For judicious choice we must have wisdom. Secondly, one must have wisdom to distinguish between what is real and what is unreal. Without wisdom the right knowledge cannot be gained.

Patience (Titiksha) is another quality one must cultivate in order for the right knowledge to be dawn. It is like going in an automobile which does not have shock absorbers. In this complex world of people with different attitudes, and mannerism, we expect others to behave or talk as we expected. If this did not happen, we lose our patience, and show our irritation or anger. Without patience knowledge cannot be gained.

Faith (Shraddha) is another quality most important in acquiring knowledge. Just like, if you don't have faith in the doctor your disease will not be cured by the medicines prescribed by him; if you don't have faith in the teacher (Guru) and the Scriptures, you will not gain knowledge. First you have to choose the right teacher who has the knowledge, and conversant with the scriptural texts, where the Highest Knowledge is depicted.

Determination (Mumukshatva) is the last discipline required for experiencing the Bliss. One must be convinced and determined to enjoy Bliss in the present life, and seek liberation from the endless cycle of birth and death. Suppose a person who is not convinced of life after death, need not seek liberation. He is not qualified. One must be determined and make a resolve, after firm conviction, to experience Bliss which is billion times more than the happiness we have experienced on different occasions. One must realise the fact that the world is not real, the attachments with kith and kin, and the material possessions are impositions by the mind and illusory in nature, and develop the attitude of detachment. For this attitude to progress, one must learn philosophy which teaches 'Vyragya' or detachment. Two most important requirements for receiving the Self-knowledge are Wisdom and detachment.

10.3 PROCESS OF IMPARTING KNOWLEDGE

The process of imparting the knowledge about the Ultimate Reality is a special method adopted by most teachers; it is known as process of negation or elimination one after the other, since it is not possible to name or describe the Ultimate Reality. After removing what is not real, what remains is only Real. Let us apply this process of negation to world or the universe we see.

The observable universe comprises of only four things: space, time, matter and living beings. Before analysing each one of them, let us define what is Real. Most religions refer God as Real. By analysing, it can be proved that God must be eternal. That is It must be formless and nameless, since we have proved that anything that has name and form cannot be eternal. Eternal also means not having taken birth and exists all the time. It must not undergo any change or divisible into parts. Let us assume, for the time being, that space, time, matter and living beings are the creations of God. By proving that spacc time, matter and human beings are not real, we will be left with so called God which is Real.

10.4 SPACE AND SPACE-TIME

Let us consider space. It is very difficult to imagine space. Anything that grows in size must have space to accommodate. For example, a plant cannot grow in height or size if there is no space. When a dining hall is full of people, we say there is no space and we have to wait until someone leaves giving space to us to dine. To describe the position of an aeroplane, at a particular instant, we have to specify its longitude, latitude and altitude. Generally speaking space has three dimensions; we can say length, width and height, and mathematically speaking, the x, y and z coordinates. When Newton formulated his gravitational theory and laws of motion, he assumed a three-dimensional static universe in which time flows at a constant rate. These views have to be changed following Einstein's Relativity theories. It was experimentally verified that time does not flow uniformly in space. Time is not absolute and flow of time depends on the speed of the object and also objects position in space such as gravitational field. For example, as the speed of the object increases, the clock carried by the rocket slows down. The time also slows down if it is closer to a black hole.

Time is not absolute, but only relative; for example, what is present time on earth at one place is different at different locations. It is morning for people on the east while it is night for those living on the west side of the spinning earth. Similarly, what is the time now on a distant planet in faraway galaxy has no meaning. For another instance, when we see a light from a distant galaxy which is 150 light-years away from the earth, the light must have started its journey 150 years back to reach us at the present moment.

Let us explore space further; there was no space before the creation of this universe. This space can expand as well as contract. Space is elastic like rubber. We all know the universe has been expanding ever since the Big bang started. Before the big bang there was no space, time or matter. When we say the universe is expanding, one gets doubt into where it is expanding. Unless space itself expandable, the expansion of the universe is not possible.

Einstein not only dispensed away Newton's concepts of absolute space and absolute time, but he went further and expressed the view that space and time are intimately connected. Further, the notions of space and time may be interchanged.

Suppose in a dining car of a superfast train, two people sitting at the two extreme ends of the dining car light their cigars at the same time; to an observer in the dining car the two events are simultaneous, but to an observer on a stationary railway platform, it would appear as if the two events have taken place at two different times. Similarly, it can be proved two events occurring at the same place, in a speeding train, but at two different times, appear to the ground observer as if the two events occurred at two different places. These concepts can be well understood with the help of a space-time diagrams, with three dimensional space along x-axis and time along y-axis.

Einstein, through his relativity and gravitational theories, established that space and time are interchangeable terms. "Events occurring in the same *place* but at different *times* in a moving system will be considered by a ground observer as occurring at two different *places.*" Now, following the Einstein's reciprocity of space and time, we can replace in the above statement the word *place* by the word *time* and vice versa. Now the above statement can be written as "Events occurring at the same *time* but at two different places, in a moving system, will be considered by the ground observer as occurring at two different *times.*

This new reality that space and time are mere physical constructs, and have to be combined into a new entity called 'space-time', because the equations of relativity theory show that both the space and time coordinates of any event must get mixed together by the mathematics, in order to accurately describe what we see. Because space consists of 3 dimensions, and time is 1-dimensional, space-time must, therefore, be a 4-dimensional continuum. It is believed to be a 'continuum' because so far as we know, there are no missing points in space or instants in time, and both can be subdivided without any apparent limit in size or duration. So, physicists now routinely consider our world to be embedded in this 4-dimensional Space-Time continuum, and all events, places, moments in history, actions and so on are described in terms of their location in Space-Time.

In relativistic contexts, time cannot be separated from the three dimensions of space, because the observed rate at which time passes, for an object, depends on the object's velocity relative to the observer and also on the strength of gravitational field; gravity slows time for an object as seen by an observer outside the field.

In our solar system, the sun is at the centre and all planets move around it in elliptical orbits. But, according to Einstein, all planets, including earth, follow a straight line motion not elliptical paths. The mass of the sun will warp or form a curved shape to the space-time fabric of the universe, around it, just like when we place a cricket ball at the centre on a flat rubber sheet, will form a bell shape at the centre. Now if one drops a marble on the sheet, it will go round and round the cricket ball. This is only an analogy, but the fact remains that earth is going along a straight path, but due to the presence of the Sun the space is curved or warped around it and so to the observer it appears as though the earth follows an elliptical path around it.

Since we do not know perfectly about the shape of the universe, how many dimensions are needed to describe the universe is still an open question. Some speculative theories include additional dimensions. For example, theories such as string theory predicts space with 11 dimensions, 10 spatial one temporal. According to Einstein, gravity is nothing but geometry of space-time. As we know geometry is only a construction by the mind. Therefore the space or space-time continuum is only a projection by the mind.

10.5 TIME

Time is a measure in which events can be ordered from the past through the present into the future, and also the measure of durations of events and the intervals between them. Time is often referred to as the fourth dimension, along with the three spatial dimensions.

Time has long been a major subject of study in religion, philosophy and science, but defining it in a manner applicable to all fields without circularity has consistently eluded scholars. Nevertheless, diverse fields such as business, industry, sports, the sciences, and the performing arts, all incorporate some notion of time into their respective measuring systems. Some simple definitions of time include "time is what clocks measure," which is a problematically vague and self-referential definition that utilizes the device used to measure the subject as the definition of the subject, and "time is what keeps everything from happening at once," which is without substantive meaning in the absence of the definition of simultaneity in the context of the limitations of human sensation, observation of events, and the perception of such events.

Two contrasting viewpoints on time divide many prominent philosophers. One view is that time is part of the fundamental structure of the universe – a dimension independent of events, in which events occur in a sequence. Sir Isaac Newton subscribed to this view and hence it is sometimes referred as Newtonian time. The opposing view is that *time* does not refer to any kind of "container" that events and objects "move through," nor to any entity that "flows," but it is, instead, forms part of a fundamental intellectual structure (together with space and number) within which humans sequence and compare events. This second view, in the tradition of Gottfried Leibniz and Immanuel Kant holds that *time* is neither an event nor a thing, and thus it is not itself measurable nor can it be travelled.

Time is one of the seven fundamental physical quantities in both the International System of Units and International System of Quantities. Time is used to define other quantities—

such as velocity; so defining time in terms of such quantities would result in circularity of definition. An operational definition of time, wherein one says that observing a certain number of repetitions of one or another standard cyclical event (such as the passage of a free-swinging pendulum) constitutes one standard unit such as the *second* highly useful in the conduct of both advanced experiments and everyday affairs of life.

The operational definition leaves aside the question whether there is something called time, apart from the counting activity just mentioned, that flows and that can be measured. Investigations of a single continuum called space-time bring questions about *space* into questions about *time*, questions that have their roots in the works of early students of natural philosophy. Furthermore, it may be that there is a subjective component to time, but whether or not time itself is "felt," as a sensation, or is a judgment, is a matter of debate.

Temporal measurement has occupied scientists and technologists as a prime motivation in navigation and astronomy. Periodic events and periodic motion have long served as standards for units of time. Examples include the apparent motion of the sun across the sky, the phases of the moon, the swing of a pendulum, and the beat of a heart. Currently, the international unit of time, the *second* is defined in terms of radiation emitted by caesium atoms. Time is also of significant social importance, having economic value ("time is money") as well as personal value, due to an awareness of the limited time in each day and in human life spans.

The time scale of the universe is very long compared to that of human life. It was therefore not surprising that until recently, the universe was thought to be essentially static, and unchanging in time. Today, the situation is different, however, when it was realised that the universe is not static, but expanding. Galaxies are moving steadily apart from each other as measured by red shift. This means that they were closer together in the past. Time, after the Big Bang, will not depend on anything that may have happened before, because the deterministic laws that govern the universe will break down in the Big Bang. The universe evolved from the Big Bang, completely independently of what it was like before. Even the amount of matter in the universe, can be different to what it was before the Big Bang, as the Law of Conservation of Matter, will break down at the Big Bang.

Since events before the Big Bang have no observational consequences, one may as well cut them out of the theory, and say that time began at the Big Bang. In order to discuss observations in cosmology, it is helpful to draw a diagram of events in space and time, with time going upward, vertical axis, and the three dimensional space represented along the horizontal axis which are known as Feynman diagrams.

Let us consider whether, *Time* has any basis for its existence. We cannot spend an hour without looking at the watch. The concept of time, as we all know, has been derived based on the time of one rotation of the earth around its own axis forming day and night. People needed to know the distinction between pairs of events occurring. So the water clock, the sand clock, mechanical clock, digital clock, atomic clock, and optical clocks with higher and higher accuracies have been devised.

We need time to distinguish between the past, present, and probably future. If we analyse closely we come to the conclusion it is the work of our mind. Consider *yesterday*. It has passed, and where it exists, in our mind, in the form of memory of certain events that have taken place yesterday. Now consider *future*. Where does it exist?. It is yet to come. It exists in our mind only in the form of some expectations or some activities planned in our mind. Therefore future does not exist except it is our imagination. Now let us consider the *present*. First we have to define present. Is it a day, an hour or a second?

Even a second that has passed will become the past, and the next second will be our future, only current one second is our present. So the span of present is one second. Now imagine we divide this second further into nanoseconds or Pico seconds, where we stand at the present. It is a figment of our imagination. Therefore *time* has no basis for its existence; it is a mental creation; a creation by mind.

10.6 MATTER

Matter is a substance that occupies physical space. According to modern physics, matter consists of various types of particles, each with mass and size. Matter has two properties: inertia and gravity.

Electron, proton and neutron are considered particles which constitute an atom. Protons and neutrons form the nucleus of an atom, and electrons revolve around the nucleus. There are more than 100 different kinds of atoms, each kind constituting a unique chemical element. A combination of atoms forms a molecule. Atoms and/or molecules can join together to form a compound..

Matter can exist in several states, also called phases. The three most common states are known as solid, liquid and gas. A single element or compound of matter might exist in more than one of the three states, depending on the temperature and pressure. Less familiar states of matter include *plasma* and Bose-Einstein condensate. These states occur under special conditions.

Different kinds of matter can combine to form substances that may not resemble any of the original ingredients. For example, hydrogen (a gaseous element) and oxygen (another gaseous element) combine to form water (a liquid compound at room temperature). The process of such combination is called a chemical reaction. A chemical reaction involves interactions between the electrons of the atoms, but does not affect the nuclei of the atoms.

In some situations, matter is converted into energy by atomic reactions, also known as nuclear reactions. This type of reaction is fundamentally different from the chemical reaction because it involves changes in the nuclei of atoms. The most common example of an atomic reaction is the hydrogen fusion that occurs inside the sun. The immense pressure inside the stars, forces atoms of hydrogen come together to form atoms of helium. In this process, some of the mass is converted to energy according to the formula discovered by Einstein, $E = mc^2$, where E is the energy in joules, m is the mass in kilograms and c is the speed of light, which is approximately 2.99792×10^8 meters per second in a vacuum.

In recent years, scientists have confirmed the existence of a substance called *antimatter*. The electron has an antiparticle twin called a *positron,* with equal mass but opposite electric charge. Similarly, the proton has an antimatter twin called an antiproton, and the neutron has an antimatter twin called an antineutron. If a particle of matter encounters its antiparticle, both are converted entirely to energy according to the above formula. Small amounts of antimatter have been isolated in laboratory conditions, but no one has yet succeeded in creating a controlled a matter/antimatter reaction, or even an uncontrolled reaction of significant size.

Before the 20th century, the term "matter" included ordinary matter composed of atoms and excluded other energy phenomena such as light or sound. This concept of matter may be generalized from atoms to include any objects having mass even when it is at rest, but this is ill-defined because an object's mass can arise from its (possibly massless) constituents' motion and interaction energies. For example, photon, the particle of light, has no mass, but it has momentum, and it can knock of an electron from its orbit in an atom. Thus, matter does not have a universal definition, nor is it a fundamental concept in physics today. Matter is also used loosely as a general term for the amount of substance that makes up all observable physical objects.

All the objects from everyday life that we can bump into, touch or squeeze are composed of atoms. By contrast, massless particles, such as photons, are not considered matter, because they have neither rest mass nor volume. However, not all particles with rest mass have a classical volume, since fundamental particles such as quarks and leptons (sometimes equated with matter) are considered "point particles" with no effective size or volume. A proton and a neutron each comprises of three quarks. Nevertheless, quarks and leptons together make up "ordinary matter," and their interactions contribute to the effective volume of the composite particles that make up ordinary matter.

Matter should not be confused with mass, as the two are not quite the same in modern physics. For example, mass is a conserved quantity, which means that its value is unchanging through time, within a closed systems. However, matter is *not* conserved in such systems, although this is not obvious in ordinary conditions on Earth, where matter is approximately conserved. Still, the special theory of relativity shows that matter may disappear by conversion into energy, even inside a closed systems, and it can also be created from energy, within such systems. However, because *mass* (like energy) can neither be created nor destroyed, the quantity of mass and the quantity of energy remain the same during a transformation of matter (which represents a certain amount of energy) into non-material (i.e., non-matter) energy. This is also true in the reverse transformation of energy into matter. Therefore, mass and energy together is conserved in a closed system.

Different fields of science use the term matter in different ways, and sometimes incompatible. Some of these ways are based on loose historical meanings, from a time when there was no reason to distinguish mass and matter. As such, there is no single universally agreed scientific meaning of the word "matter." Scientifically, the term "mass" is well-defined, but "matter" is not. Sometimes in the field of physics "matter" is simply equated with particles that exhibit rest mass (i.e., that cannot travel at the speed of light), such as quarks and leptons. However, in both physics and chemistry, matter exhibits both wave-like and particle-like properties, the so-called wave–particle duality.

Now let us consider the question of *matter*. Scientists are yet to establish how a particle has got its mass. For example there are many particles without mass. A photon, for example has no mass and therefore it can travel at the speed of light. Recent discovery of so called 'God' particle is expected to reveal how a particle acquired mass. Any particle that has mass cannot travel at the speed of light. Matter can be transformed into different shapes depending on their properties like malleability and elasticity. According to Relativity theory the mass of the object increases exponentially with the speed of the object. Similarly, the length of an object shrinks as the speed of the object increases. Also time shrinks as speed increases. This means space, time and matter can expand or contract depending on the speed of the object.

All subatomic particles, according to quantum mechanics, are neither particles nor waves. It's nature is decided by the observer who decides what experiment he devises. Therefore, the nature and existence of matter depends on the mind.

From what all said about space, time and matter, they can be resolved into mind or consciousness:

Matter is regarded as atomic rhythm,

Rhythm is regarded as geometry,

Geometry is regarded as space,

Space is regarded as time, and

Time is regarded as Consciousness.

10.7 WHO AM I?

As mentioned earlier, the world around us comprises of Space, Time, Matter and Living beings. We have established that space, time and matter have no support for their existence. Now our attention must be drawn to understanding the living beings. It is simple to do research on oneself rather than considering all living being at the same time. The knowledge that resulted in the realisation of "who am I?, has been termed as self-knowledge. We have proved that in the universe, space, time and matter are nothing but mind's precepts; there is no knowledge higher than the self-knowledge. The self-knowledge is the experience of understanding or realising everything in the universe around us, including ourselves, as pure *Consciousness.* It is not an object that can be sighted; it cannot be imagined since it is not manifested. It is Absolute. It is beyond body, senses, mind and intellect. This experience of Absolute makes the entire universe disappear as mere illusion.

The absolute cannot be taught or explained in words. The method of imparting this knowledge followed by great Rishis to the students involved a process of elimination or negation of things which are not absolute. We can explain this with an analogy to the work of a sculpture. A sculpture is making a statue of Mahatma Gandhi, out of a stone. This he does it by chiselling out unwanted material from the stone block. The image of the final statue is ingrained in his mind, and he gradually removes material which is not part of that image in his mind. Finally, a beautiful statue is realised by him. A similar method is adopted by the enlightened teacher to the disciplined student.

We adopted the same method of negation in proving that space, time and matter are not absolute. Now we apply the same method to understand ourselves to discover our true nature.

The question - answer format is a great way to teach and learn. This requires diligent involvement of the student in his quest for knowledge and an equally diligent involvement by the teacher who guides the student. The teacher must be an enlightened being having learnt the Ultimate Knowledge. The method of imparting the knowledge to his student is as old as Vedas which evolved even when there were no written scriptures available. The student gets associated with the teacher and does service to the teacher who understood the Reality. The teacher first helps him how to purify his body and mind from all delusions, and then imparts the knowledge step by step. The student is made to understand the importance of listening with concentration. The student learns by constant questioning, and contemplation on the answers.

This three-step process of learning, are referred as, 'Sravana', 'Manana' and 'Nidhidhyasana' respectively known as listening to the teacher with concentration, contemplating on it repeatedly, and at the same time analysing and understanding.

The teacher, imperceptibly recognises the pattern of thinking by the student, and continually brings the student to path of Right Knowledge. This unique method adopted in ancient India makes them non-dogmatic. The freedom to approach the teacher in person and ask questions is the right atmosphere in which the human grows and rises to height of his Guru.

For getting this knowledge, one must practice concentration, meditation and contemplation. The student, who is seriously interested in acquiring this highest knowledge, must fulfil certain qualifications; just like, if a student wants to become professional doctor eligible to practice, he must pass specified examinations.

An individual, in order to interact with this world, uses three of his instruments; body, senses like mouth and ears, and mind. All bad things in the world also enter through these same three instruments. He accumulates all sins through these instruments; so he has to ensure they are clean at all times. For cleansing his body, he has to perform his prescribed duties for himself and for his family: taking bath, performing rituals, offering prayers to his family God, taking care of his family members, and aged parents. For cleansing his mouth and ear, he must read holy books daily, and hear spiritual discourses from learned scholars. For cleansing his mind, one has to meditate for few minutes focusing on the image of God or candle light, etc.

Tamasik people must undertake social programmes, even with a selfish motive, in order to generate in them the dynamism of Rajas. The Rajasik people should learn to act in a spirit of selflessness in order to generate the brilliance of Sattvik in them. The Sattvik people must involve in 'actionless -actions' to reach the larger awakening into higher Consciousness in them.

The human body can be broadly divided into five parts. The physical body, the life force, the mind, the intellect and the happy state we enjoy during deep-sleep. In the next chapter, these five parts, taken one at a time is negated and proved not real, leaving the student to experience the Infinite Consciousness.

11

SELF-KNOWLEDGE

The story of Nachiketa, a young boy, who goes to the God of death, Yama, and seeks answers to his questions, as depicted in the Katha Upanishad is important before going into the subject of self-knowledge.

Once there was a rich Brahmin who performs all types of sacrifices to please gods. But since he is arrogant and very much after fulfilling his personal desires, but nothing is materialising. He is very much irritated. He had a son by name, Nachiketa. He observed his father is giving away old and diseased cows, in charity, to the poor, and so he is not able to please the gods. One day, Nachiketa approaches his father, and asks him when he will give away him in charity. For this the father got angry with his son and says,' I shall sacrifice you to the God Yama'.

The boy, Nachiketa took his father's word seriously and went to hell in search of Yama. But he had to wait for three days to meet Yama. Finally when he met Yama, the lord of the hell, Yama, apologises to the Brahmin boy for making him wait for three days without offering him food or water. As a compensation, he sanctioned three boons to Nachiketa. Nachiketa asks for removal of anger from the mind of his father, and as a second boon he asks Yama to name the sacrifice by which a man can ascend to heaven after death. God Yama sanctioned both the boons, and asks the boy about his third boon.

Nachiketa asks an answer for his question as the third boon. He asks, what is death?, what happens to the man after his death? Yama was puzzled about this question as many gods are trying to find answer, while this boy is asking him directly. For this the God of Death, Yama, said, "ask for a kingdom, gold, cattle, elephants, chariots and horses. Ask for sons and grandsons who live for hundred years. Ask for wealth and long life, and enjoy life with all the pleasures you can imagine, but don't insist answer for this question."

But, Nachiketa was very determined to find the answer for his question, and said, "Keep all these riches, with you, which are temporary, and eat away all my energies. Man cannot be satisfied by wealth, and it does not come with us when we die. So keep them all with you and please enlighten me on my doubt."

The god of death, impressed by the wisdom of the young boy, starts his teaching instructions thus: 'perfection is one thing, while enjoyment is another; these two having different ends, engage men differently. He who chooses perfection becomes pure, while the one who chooses enjoyment misses his true end. Both perfection and enjoyment present themselves to the man; the wise man, having examined both, distinguishes one from the other. The wise man chooses perfection, being superior to enjoyment, but the foolish man chooses enjoyment for the pleasure of his body and senses. O Nachiketa, having thought upon things which give sensual pleasures, you wisely abandoned them." The Death God, Yama, proceeds to teach Nachiketa.

"What becomes of a man when he dies? "This wise One never dies, is never born; Unborn, Eternal-this ancient One can never be destroyed with the destruction of the body. If the slayer thinks he is the slayer, and if the slain thinks he is slain, know that both are ignorant, not understood the Truth, for the

Self is neither a slayer nor a slain." The story tells us to be wise, and choose the right path.

The *Self*, which a wise man seeks is covered by five layers: The Gross physical body, Prana or breath, the Mind, the Intellect, and Joy or happiness. In order to know about oneself, one has to systematically analyse and eliminate these layers, one by one, until one is left to find where the feeling of "I" "me" and "mine" originate. The same process of elimination is employed here.

The 'Atma,' the individual self, Soul or Jiva, whatever name it is referred, must be understood as nothing but the reflection of the Pure Consciousness in the Subtle body, which identifies itself with the Gross body. This Self is covered by five layers or sheaths or koshas.

11.1 THE HUMAN BODY (ANNA-MAYA)

Our gross body constitutes the first layer, which is known as 'Anna-Maya kosha' or sheath that envelopes and hides our true nature from being known or revealed to us.

Anna-Maya is also known as food sheath, and is made up of the five elements, space, air, fire, water and earth. It has a beginning and an end. The body is born at one point and dies at another point of time. It is inert, made of parts. Though the body undergoes decay and death, you are not the body; you are the witness of this body.

When a child is born, who is responsible? If one asks the parents, they say they are only instrumental, and not creators of the child; they do not know the gender of the child or when exactly it will be born. Consider, for example, a watch maker; he knows each and every part of the watch, and can explain how it works. Since he is the creator of the watch, he will be able to explain every part, and how it works. This is not the case with parents of a child. The parents do not know what transformation taken place and how the child is born.

The individual in the mother's womb, as it first enters, has no shape. The sperm of the father meets the egg of the mother to form the foetus. This happens after millions of sperm cells are rejected and killed before one single sperm succeeds in forming the foetus. These sperms have life when they are with the father, but once they leave the father and enter the mother's organ, they all get killed within 24 hours, except one. This seed is responsible for the formation of the foetus, and the foetus grows month by month, and finally it takes human form in the 7th month. Just like we are not aware how our finger nails grow, or hair on our head grows, the foetus grows inside the mother's womb.

This is similar to how a seed grows into a tree. The child is given a name only after birth. The child did not have name or proper shape until it is born out of the womb. Did the child exist before it entered mother's womb? Yes, it exists with father, in the form of sperm. Where from the sperm formed? The sperm grows from the food taken by the father. Where from the food came? Food came from the plants. Where from the plants come from? For the plant to produce food by photosynthesis, five elements are needed; earth, water, fire, air, and space.

Where from these elements came? They are created in the process of creation of the universe. From the Iswara, with the help of Maya, Hiranyagarbha (Vishnu) came into existence. From the novel of Vishnu, Virat (Brahma) is born, and from Brahma, 'pancha bhoota' (the five elements) came into existence. From the pancha bhoota, the living beings and non- living world is created, through a process known as 'Quintuplicating' or 'Panchikaranm'. According to this process, the world is originated from one Reality that exists which is Brahman. Brahman transforms itself serially into the five rudimentary elements which, by admixture in different proportions, create the phenomenal world. Brahman enters into each and every thing created by Him, Thus, He is both the efficient as well as material cause of this world.

The human body is made up of primarily five elements in their pure form and as well as their modifications. This is easy to comprehend. Whatever parts that get dissolved in the earth when the human body is burnt or buried must be known as formed from the earth.

The five elements are present always in every one of us. Our body consists of trillions of cells, and each cell consists of 65% water (water element). There is heat (fire element) in our body that maintains the body temperature at 37 degree Celsius; if this temperature increases too much or decreases too much we are dead. Similarly, the air in our lungs must be present all the time (air element). The space is everywhere and we cannot grow without space (space element) Thus all the five elements are present in our body all the time.

Therefore, the gross body is formed from the combination of the five elements in their modified forms and since it is inert it carries with it the characteristic known as Tamas Guna. The subtle body comprising of inner senses, prana, mind, intellect and ego, is also formed, in a similar way from the five elements, but in their purest form, combining with three Gunas of nature: *Sattva, Rajas and Tamas.* For example, the sense organs came from water and Rajas Guna; Prana (life force) came from fire and Sattva Guna; mind formed from air and Sattva Guna and intellect formed from Space and Sattva Guna. Ego is formed from only ignorance.

The journey of the child, if taken backwards, we reach the creation of the universe. By similar reasoning, we can say the child exists even after its death. Till the death, the child grows in size and weight, passing through different stages of life; childhood, youth, adulthood and old age. An individual knows he has grown from his childhood into old age. The question is who is the knower? Obviously not the body; since it underwent changes. There must be something which did not undergo any change to observe changes, and who is the witness to the bodily changes?

Whenever any part of our gross body, say hand or leg, is severed from the rest of the body it does not respond to any stimuli. Only when they form part of the body they carry sensory information like touch, hot or cold, smooth or rough, etc. to the brain. The whole body, when we goes to sleep, will not respond to any stimuli. This proves that what we are seeking *Self* is not the physical Gross body or Annamya kosha, comprising of bones, sense organs, flesh, veins, nerves, blood, marrow, etc.

11.2 LIFE FORCE (PRANA-MAYA)

Pranayama sheath or kosha is also known as the vital Sheath and is a product of five elements and Rajas Guna. It also has a beginning and end. It is inert, and therefore, Self is not the Pranayama kosha or sheath, but it is only a witness to its functioning, since we can observe the 'prana' or air we breathe entering and leaving through our nostrils.

The air we breathe in is known as Prana. When this Prana enters the body through the nostrils, it gets divided into five parts: *prana, apana, vyana, udana and samana*. Breathing air in, is known as prana, and air we breathe out is called apana. These two keep our body run like a machine. The air transfers oxygen to the blood. The blood circulates entire body. The oxygen that is carried to the entire body is called 'vyana', the oxygen that goes to the brain is called 'udana', and the oxygen in the lungs is known as 'samana'.

The body and mind are related, and they effect each other. The way we breathe, has profound effect on the internal organs and ultimately the mind. For example, when we experience anger or fear, we breathe faster, sometimes we express our anger by clinching our fist or grinding our teeth. We can imagine that reverse of this process also, is possible. If we can control breathe and reduce its rate we control our anger. Therefore, the link between body and mind is the breath or Prana.

There are three main veins or *nadis* in our body that life force moves through them: *Ida*, *pingala* and *sushumna*. The air that moves through the left nostril is known as 'ida', the air that flows through the right nostril is known as 'pingala', and the place where both meet is called the 'sushumna'. The sushumna nadi is the central vein. There are 10001 veins in our body through which life force moves in our body. The vibrations of the life force make the mind vibrate and vice versa. The Ida nadi or breath through the left nostril regulates our thoughts, while, the pingala or the breathe through the right nostril will regulate energy in our body. The central nadi or sushumna is vein where the ida and pingala meet is known as knowledge centre.

Proper coordination of these three nadis through the practice of Pranayama leads to good health, strength, long life wisdom and peace of mind. The process of pranayama teaches as how to regulate our breath. That is, it depends on how long we inhale, how long we hold the breathe, and how long we exhale.

When the body undergoes decay and death, neither the life force nor the mind is destroyed. Here mind implies four of its functions, mind, intellect, ego and memory. These four together form the subtle body and becomes the seed for next birth. The prana leaves the body joins with prana outside. However, prana is not eternal. Because it is formed and energises the body; when it leaves the body, the body loses its breathing ability. Since we observe breathing in and out, it can be concluded that 'prana' or life force is not the 'Self', we are seeking.

11.3 MIND (MANO-MAYA)

The mano-maya is also known as mental sheath and is a product of the Air element, in its pure form, combined with Sattva Guna. It has also beginning and end, it is inert, and it is an effect. So, you are not the mental sheath or mano-maya kosha, but only a witness to it.

According to scientists, nearly 73000 thoughts invade our brain every day. Most of these thoughts are irrelevant, unconnected and involuntary. So controlling and regulating thoughts through practice of yoga, known as *pranayama*, is very important in controlling mind.

We have discussed already the nature of mind and its three states of consciousness. According to the Oxford dictionary, the mind has been defined as the seat of consciousness, thought, volition and feeling. We see how far this definition holds well.

Mind is a very complex thing to understand; because, the flow of thoughts is mind, and the observer of these thoughts is also the same mind. Mind can create friends as well as enemies. We compare our behaviour with that of others. If other's behaviour matches with ours, they become our friends, otherwise they become enemies. This comparison is the root cause for creating friends or enemies.

Life becomes beautiful if we learnt what to remember and what to forget. We must forget events and people who made us sad; and remember people who made us happy. One must learn to exorcise those bad memories. Dredging up and holding on to those bad memories, we will be making them rankle in the mind forever. Therefore, we must cultivate the habit of forget and forgive. If God forgives all, we too must forgive others. Otherwise it amounts to setting us as higher tribunal than Him.

Mind only binds us to the world and people around, and creates misery; and the same mind is the source of Bliss and cause for liberation. All functions of the mind are absent during deep-sleep. This is my house, these are my kith and kin, etc. are the thoughts that bind us in the waking state. If one understands the working of the mind, he gains control over the mind. It is to understand how the mind and our personality are connected. When the child is born, it is the mother who starts communicating with it. Then she slowly introduces her husband as father to the child, then other family members, uncles and grandparents. This is how the relationships are established, layer by layer and we are bound to the family. Therefore all our relationships are nothing but superimpositions in our mind.

Secondly, let us analyse how we change our behaviour and conduct when we interact with different people in the same family. For example, same man talks and behaves in a particular way with his wife, assuming the role as a husband expressing love. Same man when he meets his mother, he talks differently, expressing his affection and enquiring about her health. Again, the same man takes up the role as a father, when he sees his son, and scolds him for not doing his homework. Likewise, each individual enacts a role in this world of drama. If he is aware of his changing roles, each experience will be pleasant to him. He must always remember he is only an actor. On the other hand, if he gets entangled in the family web inviting all worries, problems and make his life miserable in solving all the problems. If he understands his different roles he has to play, and do his job as a responsibility, he does not feel the burden.

In deep-sleep state, the person is extremely happy, and this state of happiness is same for all human beings, irrespective of his health, wealth. A beggar sleeping on a footpath, or a rich man sleeping on a cushioned bed in an air-conditioned room, will experience the same happiness. If one can maintain the same happy state during waking state in the day also, the world looks beautiful and we feel happy for ever. This is the simple secret behind the feel-happy mood always.

Just like all activities of the world begin after the sun rises, the world comes into existence in the light of the mind. Anything other than the Absolute Consciousness falls in the domain of the mind. That is, entire cosmos including the space, time, life force and the mind are but Mind. The entire world is created by the mind. There is nothing real or unreal in the world; it is the mind that makes something appear as real or unreal.

The mind is nothing; it is merely a name of the Absolute consciousness that imagines or pulsates out of its free will; just like we have no control over our dreams.

The world gets created like the illusory water is created by a mirage. The mind is just a will, and the nature of the will is to pulsate or vibrate. From the pulsation arise the actions and consequences. The gross world comes into existence when the mind vibrates, and ceases to exist when the mind stops vibrating. The mind is just an imagination; the world it creates is called an illusion (Maya). When the will becomes reinforced, the mind experiences the external objects as real. The entire world is anchored in the mind.

We hear a patient undergoing brain operation without anaesthesia; because it is feared he might lose his ability to speak if anaesthesia is given. So, the patient was playing guitar during the operation. In another instance, a woman in UK got her leg amputed without anaesthesia. How such things are possible, unless it is possible to switch on or off the mind so that pain is not felt.

Mind is the link between the phenomenal world and the Absolute Consciousness. Everything depends on how we control our mind, and how we reduce the number of unconnected thoughts that pass through every day. The mind can be controlled only in future, but the future depends on our desires; and desires are nothing but the mind. We fall in the trap. Just as we control a naughty boy in the house, by keeping an eye on him, the mind can be controlled of unruly thoughts just by observing. Unless the mind is quietened, the desires cannot be extinguished. The desires cannot be extinguished until the Absolute knowledge dawns. The body is the seed of the individual self, the mind is the seed of the body, and desire is the seed of the mind.

Actions are expressions of thoughts, and they are the disturbances in the mind caused by desires, which in turn, generated by ignorance. The extrovertedness of the mind, with its outgoing tendencies along with ego is 'Bondage', whereas when the mind and the ego turns towards the Self, it is 'Freedom'. The mind does not function during deep sleep, and the next day we wake up and say we had a sound sleep. It is clear from the above discussion that mind is not the Self.

11.4 INTELLECT (VIJNANA-MAYA)

Vijnana-Maya is also known as intellect sheath and is a product of Akas element, in its pure form, combined with Sattva Guna. It too, has a beginning and end, it is inert and it is an effect. Therefore you are not the intellect sheath or Vijnana-Maya kosha, but only a witness.

From the Upanishad point of view, to know the things through the sense organs is called *Vijnana;* acquiring special knowledge through analysis and contemplation is known as *jnana*; and the knowledge about the Supreme Consciousness is known as *Prajna.*

In order to teach true knowledge to the student who is a beginner to spirituality, the process of elimination is generally employed by the teacher. Some people call it the process of negation. Since the entire universe is the object of our cognition, the teacher eliminate the universe or the world, consisting of space, time and matter, first by saying it cannot be the Absolute Consciousness or Brahman.

Then the teacher takes up the human being, comprising of five sheaths or layers namely, Anna-Maya, Pranayama, Mano-Maya, Vijnana-Maya, and Ananda-Maya, eliminating one after another. Here the teacher argues how the Vijnana-Maya is not the Supreme Self.

I am intelligent, I am knowledgeable, I am ignorant, etc. are the feelings arise due to our intellect. On a Sunday evening, I don't know what to do; the mind proposes different alternatives like going to a restaurant, movie or take a book to read. It is our intellect that decided one way or the other.

All knowledge is gained by one who wishes to know and an object, gross or abstract, that is to be known or inquired into. In the pursuit of knowledge, the inquirer uses the senses and the intellect. The intellect functions with the help of language and logic in order to experience and to express the knowledge that has been gained.

In the absence of an object of cognition, we cannot begin our inquiry; just because we cannot inquire about "Nothing." We use sense organs to understand and analyse what we see or observe in the universe. We use eyes to know the colour of an object, and no other senses. If we are deaf, we cannot enjoy music.

For acquisition of knowledge, there must be three-fold association; the knower (subject), the known (object) and the process of knowing through the senses. But it is the mind and the intellect that acquire the knowledge by processing the information provided by the senses. When the mind is engaged in thinking of something else, even though we are present at a music concert, and eyes and ears are active, we cannot enjoy the music at all.

Let us see another example; suppose a man sees a singing bird perched on a tree branch. Obviously the man is seeing the bird with his two eyes and hear it singing with both the ears; the question now is whether the man seeing the bird and the man hearing its song is one and the same or two different persons. If it were two persons, how the functions of seeing and hearing taking place simultaneously. We know the eyes cannot hear and the ears cannot see; it can be concluded only one person is involved in both hearing and knowing. The question now is who is the person? Is it the body, mind, intellect or senses? Who is conscious of these acts? If we assume entire body is conscious, then each and every part of the body must be conscious; but this is not what is observed or experienced.

If we decide that our senses are conscious, this view is also not tenable since a man who becomes blind due to an accident cannot see anything. Further, if the senses carry the information, there must be someone who synthesises the information and converts it into knowledge. Therefore the knower must be different from the senses.

The conscious self is with us all the time. In fact the Self is the only thing in the world that is self- evident. So, the conscious self is beyond the intellect, and its logic and language.

The Infinite Self is the very light of Consciousness that illumines all our thoughts, and without which our intellect becomes an inert equipment of matter. Naturally the intellect cannot, by its activities, comprehend the Self, the very essence behind it. Just like the light bulb of a torch can never illumine the battery behind it. Therefore it can be concluded that the intellect is not the Self we are searching for.

11.5 HAPPY STATE (ANANDA-MAYA)

A*nanda* means happy state. Every one of us experience, during deep-sleep state, the maximum happiness. Since we are free and effortless without desires during deep sleep, we feel extreme happiness. But ignorance is present even in this state, and this state is the door way to the other two states, waking and dream state. The Ananda-Maya kosha or sheath is full of ignorance, and is an effect of past karmas. It is transient, gross and insentient. Therefore you are not the Ananda-Maya sheath, but only a witness.

Every species living on this planet strives to be comfortable, happy, and joyful. It is said, the comfort is experienced by the physical body, happiness or Ananda is enjoyed by the mind, and the bliss is experienced by the self.

Ananda in Sanskrit means *Happiness*. Every one of us have experienced some happy moments in our day to day life, but very few ponder over it. If one observes closely, the happiness we talk about lasts only for few minutes at the most. Thereafter the happiness disappears and despair or unhappiness takes its place. Thus we constantly search for happiness that lasts for few minutes. Even though happiness is a state of mind, the mind goes into the outside world searching for happiness continually.

What is the cause for the happiness? It can be anything: a good news of marriage, birth of a child, a promotion or increase in pay, acquiring a car or house we longed for it, meeting an old friend, going to a movie or eating at a restaurant, going for picnic or visiting a famous tourist place. Had any one of these provided us a lasting happiness we do not go after the materialistic goals one after another. Many youngsters imagine wealth, marriage and sex provides maximum happiness, but this also lasts only for few minutes. More and more desires start invading.

Therefore, comfort, pleasure, and happiness we get from the outside world is transient. Most youngsters express wealth alone is enough to have a happy life. If one is not healthy any amount of wealth is of no use to him. So others say health is more than wealth. However our health is not completely in our hands, though some argue do this exercise and go to that gym, etc. Still others argue if you do not dig out the past and do not worry about the future, one will be happy.

The fact is that when one desire is fulfilled we will be happy for a while. But unfortunately, desire after desire will be keep cropping up. If one of our desire is not fulfilled we will be frustrated and become angry. In some people, the severity of frustration is so strong they resort to criminal or illegal activities with a multiplied desire to acquire at any cost. The root cause for desire is the void in the mind, and the cause for this void is due to one's ignorance about his true nature.

The Ananda, one enjoys comprises of three stages, namely, 'Priyam, 'Modam' and 'Pramodam'. The happiness one derives by listening to pleasing things is known as Priyam. This can be a music, or praising words from friends or colleagues, or good news informed by someone about reward or award, etc.

The happiness one derives by seeing beautiful places, sceneries, sunset or sun rise, etc.is known as Modam. The happiness one derives by physically experiencing a happy moments such as heartily laughing at a joke, or enjoying an air-conditioned comfort after experiencing hot weather outside, etc. is known as Pramodam. Therefore happiness is short lived while Bliss is eternal. Happiness is experienced by acquiring worldly objects one desires by expending energy and wealth. The Bliss is entirely different from happiness, and can be experienced only through Self-knowledge. Virtue and vice, happiness and sorrow are the attributes of the mind, not Yourself. One who transcends, mind, good and evil, lives in True Happiness or Bliss, and therefore it is beyond the transient state of happiness.

CONCLUSION

Most of the scientists, today, believe that the universe came into existence from nothing, by accident, through a process as described by Big Bang Theory. Life and consciousness evolved from inert matter. Most of the religious scriptures around the world, on the other hand, describe the faith that the universe is created by God.

In this book, it is systematically analysed and established that both views do not stand scrutiny. There is only one Ultimate Reality, that is eternal which is of nature of Pure Consciousness that pervades everything. This illusory world is only a projection by the mind, on the Consciousness. There is no second thing exists apart from this Consciousness. This has been established by following a process known as 'negation'; that is eliminating, one by one that is not real.

We all know we are happiest during deep-sleep in the night. If this happiness can be experienced during the whole day, one can imagine how his life would be. How to realise this Supreme consciousness by the human being is elaborated further here.

Our body can be broadly divided into three parts: The Gross body, the subtle body and the Causal body. The Gross body is the one that perishes after death. As long as we live we interact and enjoy the objects of the world and comforts it provides. The gross body comprises of bones, flesh, blood vessels, lungs, heart, kidneys, liver, and all types of fluids like blood. They perish when the body is cremated or buried. But so long it is alive, it performs many tasks. The energy comes, not only from the food we eat, but by the reflection of Consciousness in the Gross body. This reflection is known as *Visva.* The Visva, whose sphere of activity is waking state whose consciousness relates to things external, who enjoys gross objects in the external world. This is sometimes referred, in the Upanishads, as first quarter of the state of mind.

The Subtle body comprises of the, mind, intellect, ego, memory. These four faculties together constitutes the subtle body. This Subtle body, after death, departs the physical body and migrates to different worlds before it takes birth again incarnating into another gross body. The subtle body carries with it all the knowledge acquired in the present life as well as previous lives, which becomes the seed for the next life. Just like we can copy all the files and information available in a computer, on to a pen drive and carry to another place.

As long as the Gross body is alive, the Subtle body performs wonderful tasks, being superior to Gross physical body. What all scientists or engineers claim to have achieved on this planet is because of this subtle body. For its activities, all the senses are illumined by the Consciousness of the Subtle body. This reflection of Consciousness in the subtle body is known as *Taijasa*. This is the second quarter whose sphere of activity is dream state, whose consciousness is internal and who enjoys subtle objects in dream.

The Causal body comprises of *Avidya* or ignorance which covers the self. This ignorance is threefold: *Malam*, can be called as impurities in the mind, due to which one can make erroneous conclusions and non-perception of reality. The second is known as Vikshepa *Sakti*, which has the power of projection and the third is known as Avarana *Sakti*, which has the power of veiling, making things appear or disappear. Unless these three defects are removed it is not possible to know the self. The Consciousness that is reflected in the Causal body is known as *Prajna.*, whose sphere of activity is deep-sleep. The sleeper does not desire any enjoyable things. Everything becomes undifferentiated, he becomes mere mass of consciousness and enjoys maximum happiness. This state of mind, known as the third quarter, becomes doorway to the other two states, waking and dream.

The fourth quarter is known as *Turiya,* which is beyond the three states, namely, waking, dream and deep-sleep. It is not describable by words. It is beyond any language or logic. Hence Upanishads seek to indicate Turiya merely through negation of its attributes…not this, not this…etc.

'AUM' is the entire universe, constituted by the three selves: Visva, Taijasa and Prajna, the human being experiences. Each letter of AUM represents each of the three conscious states, respectively, the waking, dream and deep sleep states, we experience. This analogy is explained below.

A = Visva + Gross body + waking conscious state

U = Taijasa + Subtle body + dream state

M = Prajna + Causal body + deep-sleep state

The waking-personality of 'Visva', symbolised by the letter 'A' must be resolved into 'U' (i.e. the dream personality). The subtle radiant personality of dream, the 'Taijasa' symbolised by letter 'U', must be merged into 'M' (i.e., the personality of deep-sleep). Finally, the 'Prajna' the deep-sleep Consciousness symbolised by 'M' which is the causal personality must be reduced to the Atman or Self which is of the nature of Pure Consciousness. This sort of meditation on "AUM', with full knowledge of what each letter symbolises, is recommended to reach the final state, known as *Turiya.*

It has been stated, repeatedly, in the scriptures, the conditions to be satisfied in order a person to become eligible to acquire the highest knowledge that leads to Bliss and liberation. These are: absence of desires, purity of the mind, clarity in the intellect and absence of ego.

God, who has no name or form, cannot be comprehended through reason, or logic and He possesses a glory peculiar to Himself, whose nature is Bliss, shining by itself, who is beyond (the realm) of Maya, who is known only through the Upanishadik knowledge by the process of negating what He is not.

The Supreme Consciousness that pervades the entire universe can be known only through the right knowledge. Penance, charity, chanting, fasting, worship, and meditation are in no way helpful in knowing the self. However, they purify one's actions, speech and thought and make one eligible for receiving the true knowledge. Just like light alone can remove darkness, Self-knowledge alone can remove ignorance that is preventing us to know our true nature. Due to ignorance, we see the world differently and in multiple ways.

All this objective universe consisting of three Gunas (modes of Prakriti or Nature) of the Maya which is a projection of the mind (alone), including the Jiva which is referred to as the individual self or ego, though unreal, appears real because of superimposition by the mind.

Knowers of the Self, recognise this entire universe (both subjective and objective) appears to be real, because of its being projection of their very Self; just like as those in quest of gold do not reject its modifications, in different forms of gold ornaments, because they are made from gold, so is this universe, with both of its subjective and objective aspects, conclude to be their very Self in as much as it is evolved and interpreted, too, by the Self (Brahman).

By knowledge alone misery ends; by knowledge alone ignorance is dispelled; by knowledge alone state of Bliss and liberation is attained. These are the statements by sage Vasishta. All that is visible is Pure Consciousness; this world is Consciousness alone. These are the statements by Suka Maharshi.

Experiencing Bliss and liberation is possible only by conquering the mind. That is one must understand, how the mind operates, how it pulsates and how it can be controlled. One gets the doubt, since the prana or life force stimulates the body and the senses see the world, what mind has to do with Ultimate Reality?

All methods like yoga and meditation are only preparations to quieten the mind. These methods make us more capable as how to silence the mind, and nothing more, as it is possible to silence the mind even without them. One of the features of the mind is that it survives in the extremes and disappears in the middle. Extremes here means imbalance and middle means balance. We love the worldly attractions either too much or become totally disinterested in them. These are the two extremes (hedonist or mendicant) where mind is happy. In the first extreme case, you care for yourself, and in the latter, you feel you are doing something superior. On the other hand, when you live a balanced life, the ego cannot assert itself. It is the ego that must be given up and not the selfhood.

The mind is the link between the phenomenal world and Ultimate Reality or Supreme consciousness. But the mind becomes unruly when it is not being watched. If we try to quieten the mind through any actions, it amounts to accepting that our true nature is not absolute Consciousness and something needs to be done to make it so. This also means that mind can be controlled in future, but future is nothing but a hope or desire; desire is nothing but the mind. So we fall in the trap of the mind. Since our true nature is bliss, all we need to do is to remember this fact, and become a witness. That means, one must dissociate from the mind, and watch its activities.

If the mind could be transcended, all our failures will become successes, and if not all successes will end up as failures. This is because everything in the world arises out of the mind, therefore bondage or liberation is also in the domain of the mind.

Though our true nature is Pure Consciousness, the mind makes us engage in worldly activities. The mind makes us forget our true nature which is Bliss. The same mind is responsible for waking us from deep sleep or forgetfulness. What we have to do is to understand the mind and disassociate ourselves from the pulsating and restless nature of the mind.

In deep-sleep we were extremely happy. This experience we know, after waking up. However, we cannot explain that state, because we need mind and intellect to observe that state and for us to understand. But, in deep sleep, the mind and intellect are absent or inactive. This is like catch 22 situation. The goal of every one is to experience that happy state even during waking state. How this is possible? For this we have to practice some discipline which requires using the mind and intellect. Whole thing revolves around disciplining the mind. This is possible only through gaining the right knowledge about the working of the mind and intellect. For this knowledge we have to depend on authentic scriptures and reliable Guru, who had gone through this experience.

There are only two things in this world: the inert and the Supreme Consciousness. The body, senses, mind, intellect, ego, memory, breathe, sleep are all inert or insentient and unreal and cannot be the real "I"; only that is self-effulgent is Real. The animals are not capable of acquiring this Self-knowledge; only human being is capable.

If a man tries to know everything in this world without knowing about himself, he is wasting his life. The Bliss enjoyed by the knowers of this Self-knowledge is an ample proof to drive one towards this inward journey. Many Rishis and Sages like Vasishta, Valmiki, Vyasa, Saint King Janaka, Lord Rama,

Sri Ramana Maharshi, Swami Dayananda Saraswati were enlightened souls to name a few.

When, unceasingly, the mind scans its own form, there is nothing of this kind. This direct path is open to everyone. All paths other than knowledge will not lead one to this Bliss, because they are actions in one form or the other, and the results obtained are also limited and will be in the materialistic form and are not eternal like Bliss. Secondly, we are a product of karma or action, and in that case how can different forms of actions can bring us liberation or bliss?

We are able to perceive this "infinite" universe because we are conscious of being part of it. Consciousness is the source of cognition, and therefore root of science and philosophy. Man exists in this universe, the whole universe is reflected in his consciousness, and the conscious self exists within the universe of which he is conscious and from this reflexive relation, man acquires the concept of the "infinite."

It is further established that in all our actions involving our perceptions and experiences of the physical world, our mind goes outward, whereas for experiencing the Reality, the mind must be inverted and made to undergo inward journey; and the two processes are in direct opposition. Therefore, Science which depends on perceptive or objective knowledge, takes the mind outward and hence can never lead us to comprehend Reality.

When the knowledge of the Self dawns, we learn that there are not many selves or souls that are eternal. We realise that all of us have grown out of one supreme Self and dichotomy between 'I' and 'You' is false; therefore, you are God and I am God, when the ignorance is removed. "Bliss is like a diamond protected by a snake(ego) having three heads (Satva, Rajas, and Tamas). The wise must take the sword of knowledge and behead the snake to enjoy Bliss."

When we accept that all of us are one, how can one hate another? How can the divisions between different nations, faiths, creeds and castes can exist? No one can hate another individual. We all thus become compassionate towards all fellow human beings, animals, and everything around us that move or do not move, since there is nothing other than the Self or Consciousness in this world. Now life is nothing but love and joy.

We work for sheer pleasure of it, we perform our role in this illusory world as a citizen, father, mother, son or sister, to the best of our ability. We don't love someone because he is related, but because our nature itself is love. Just as sun shines on each and every object in this world, our love extends to all flora and fauna and the entire environment.

The Advaita philosophy of Adi Sankaracharya, "The world is not Real, only Self is Truth," on which this book is based, can be understood in a simpler way.

Suppose, you are watching a movie, and you are deeply immersed and enjoying the scenes; the hero fighting the villain, and the heroine loving the hero, etc. you are immersed because you imagine yourself in the role of hero or heroine. If the movie is a tragedy where the hero and heroine die, you cry and actually tears roll down. The emotions experienced by the characters in the movie, are reflected in yourself.

Now, before going to a movie next time, you do small mental exercise or meditation, saying yourself that the characters in the movie are not real, and they are acting according to what they were directed by a director based on a script written by someone else. You can observe a change in your attitude. Also you observe the hero dies in one movie, reappears in another movie. With this knowledge when you go to a movie, you observe other spectators immersed in the movie emotionally while you remain as an observer of the movie as well as the spectators. You are constantly reminded that only the images are moving on a white screen that does not move.

When you come home, try to imagine the whole world as a big movie, and your family is a part of it. Each one plays his or her role. In your family, you enact different roles, as husband, as father, as brother etc. Similarly, when you go into the external world, you play your role as an employee or employer. In all your roles, you remain as an observer, you participate involving in your role, but without entangling yourself.

Here, you must remember one thing, in a movie all characters play their roles in accordance with directions from a single director and script writer. But in case of characters, in your family or world, are not directed not by one director, but multiple directors and script writers. These are nothing but the "karmas" of the characters accumulated over their previous births which are taking effect in their current lives. Whether happy incidents take place or tragic accidents take place, one should remain firmly as only an observer without any emotional attachments. If one can live with these convictions in real life, he will enjoy the Bliss all through his life.

The Vedanta being the science of the Self, the worldly descriptions and anecdotes presented by the Gurus, has to be viewed in their right perspective and may not have full validity in themselves, however, the student or disciple must search his own within by contemplation.

In a man of Self-realisation, it is wrong to assume that he does not recognise the world of duality and plurality around him, and his mind and intellect does not entertain thoughts. But unlike an ordinary man, he involves in worldly activities without getting entangled, and his mind is never disturbed by any confusions, since he is ever-abiding in his realisation – "I am the Infinite Self."

With the dawn of this knowledge, "I am Brahman" one gets released from the bondage of his past karmas, and be becomes 'Jivan-Mukta' which is beyond caste, creed, community, ethnicity, religion, nationality, gender and race.

Jivan-Mukta is free from desires. He moves without fear. 'For what was there to fear.' Fear comes when there is a second entity. When he realises there is no duality, where is the source for fear?

A Jivan-Mukta is free from illusions and delusions. He is free from pain and suffering. He who knows the Self, overcomes grief'. When he knows he is different from his body, where from pain comes. Neither pleasure nor pain touches him.

Wherever he moves, he sees all beings as projection of himself. He will not remain inactive, since inactivity is a characteristic of a man of Tamasik Guna, whose mind is clouded by delusions. Whatever he does, actions do not bind him. He knows his inner Self which is action-less and detached. He knows, he is not the doer, but only a witness. Having practiced spiritual discipline, he can never perform evil actions.

A liberated man who attained the blessed state is free from any doubt. The ignorance once destroyed will not come back to him.

It has been observed and explained by the sages about the behaviour of the people who realised the ultimate Reality and how they live while enjoying the state of Bliss.

Some Jivan-Muktas, according to sage Vasishta, prefer to live in mountain caves, some retire to forest, some keep travelling around the world, some prefer to meditate all the time, some become great scholars, some ruled the kingdom as kings, some give up all actions, some rejoice worldly pleasures, some renounce the world.

According to Sankara, the proponent of the Advaita philosophy, the Jivan-Mukta, at times, appears uninformed, at times with all majesty of a king, at times like misguided person, at times blissful, at times like a motionless python, at times honoured, at times disgraced, often wandering unknown. Thus lives an enlightened person in everlasting Supreme Bliss.

The enlightened Swami Dayananda Saraswati, who reached divine abode on September 23, 2015, has imparted this Self-knowledge to about 246 disciples. These include Swami Paripoornananda Saraswati, Sri Narendra Modi (present Indian Prime minister) and Acharya Prem Siddhartha to name a few.

One gets the impression that Self-knowledge is a subject of study only for the old and retired. This is grossly mistaken. For example, young Prince Rama, was imparted this Highest knowledge at the age of 16, and he faced all odds in his life spending 14 years secluded life in forests, and later he ruled the kingdom as a king. Therefore learning the Self-knowledge at a young age provides man balance of mind to face all circumstances while enjoying Bliss all the time.

If the reader of this book wants to know whether he absorbed the Self-Knowledge, these are the signs: the desires and ego must have reduced to their minimum, which reflects as anger, intolerance to people and events. He must notice the absence of fear of any events, disease or death. He does not experience dreams frequently, and lastly, he must not feel boredom at any moment. If any of these signs persist, the reader is advised to read this book again, without missing a sentence.

REFERENCES

1. Teachings of Swami Paripoornananda Saraswati on Bhagavad Gita, Atma Bodha, Kena, Prasna, Katha and Isa Upanishads; Sadhana Panchakam, Manisha Panchakam, Nirvana Shatakam and Bhajagovindam.
2. "Yoga Vasishta of Valmiki," by Dr. Kuldip Kumar Dhiman, 2014 Ukay Publishing Co, Chandigarh. (ISBN-9788175970625)
3. "Ashta Vakra Gita" by Swami Chinmayananda, Published by Chinmaya Mission Trust. (ISBN-978-8-921006-7-8)
4. "Science and Sankara in Search of Highest Truth," 1991, by the Author, Published by Bharatiya Vidya Bhavan, Mumbai.
5. "Will Science Come to an End," 1998, By the Author, Published by Allied Publishers New Delhi. (ISBN-81-70823-725-4)
6. "Mandukya Upanishad" of Sankaracharya. By Swami Gambhirananda, Advaita Ashrama, Kolkata.
7. "Brahma Sutras" of Sankaracharya, by Swami Vireswarananda, Advaita Ashrama, Kolkata.
8. "Srimad BhagavadGita," By Sistla Subbarao, TTD Publications.
9. "Panchikaranam," of Sankaracharya by Swami Jagadananda, Advaita Ashrama, Kolkata.
10. "Convergence of Science and Hindu Philosophy," 1989, by the Author, Motilal Banarsidas, Delhi.